DUANE MEHL

NO MORE FOR THE ROAD

One Man's Journey From Chemical Dependency to Freedom

Drawings by Siegfried Reinhardt

AUGSBURG PUBLISHING HOUSE
Minneapolis, Minnesota

FOR DOTTIE, DAVID, AND JENNY

NO MORE FOR THE ROAD

Contents

Preface

Once upon a time I wanted to subtitle this book, *An Addict's Journey Through the Land of Nod.* I changed my mind, but still feel attached to the phrase, "Land of Nod."

The Bible provides me the reference. Cain, you will remember, killed his brother, Abel, and then went into exile "in the land of Nod, on the east of Eden" (Genesis 4:16).

In Hebrew the word *Nod* means to move, flutter, or wander about as a vagabond. The name of Cain's land describes something of his life in that land. Like a restless spirit, he moved endlessly from place to place, finding no peace.

In English the word *nod* describes among other things the state of semi-consciousness obtained by an addict who searches for peace through just the right dosage of heroin. Similarly, barbiturate addicts may use the word to describe their own peculiar version of chemical "bliss."

Whether Cain ever nodded off in the midst of his wanderings on some ancient variety of anesthetic is a question I can't answer. I do know that many American people, living like Cain in a state of spiritual exile, spend a lot of time in their own land of nod, drinking alcohol or popping pills to bring on alteration of consciousness, reduction of anxieties, temporary euphoria and oblivion. They get bashed or stoned east of Eden and all over the place.

I know, because I spent some time myself in the land of Nod. I have written a book to reveal some of my experiences and experiences of others who have been there. I hope through the telling to discourage many of you from taking the same trip. Or I would like to reverse your present travel plans and help you leave the land of Nod forever.

To make that land real for you, I have chosen to use the language of the addict himself. For alcoholic beverages I will commonly say *booze* or *sauce* or some such word popular among drinkers. For alcoholics I may use the word *drunks*. When talking about the state of alcohol or barbiturate intoxication, I may speak of being *bombed* or *stoned* or *smashed*. If the language seems coarse to you, you will gain some idea of how coarse and degrading the experience of drug addiction can be.

Through the employment of language I hope to bring you as close to the world of drug addiction as I can. My major purpose in this book is to help you identify compassionately with the suffering drug addict.

When speaking, however, of addictive illnesses, I will also use several technical phrases almost interchangeably: chemical dependency, drug dependency, or drug addiction. The phrases refer to compulsive and abusive ingestion of habit-forming and mood-changing substances.

Alcoholism is one form of chemical dependency or of drug addiction. I will try, therefore, to distinguish alcoholism from addictions either to other mood-altering drugs, or to alcohol and other drugs in combination.

8

I write from beginning to end from the perspective of Christian faith and hope. As you might expect, however, I have in my own experience as a drug addict frequently seen my Lord and my God quite literally through a glass darkly. I cannot speak to you of the power and healing I have received through God unless I also speak of the terrible weaknesses I have experienced as a man who almost rejected God in favor of barbiturates and alcohol.

In recovery from drug addiction, the way up is the way down. Typically, we addicts fall very far from God's presence before God is able to reach us again with his outstretched fingertips. And you can never understand how intimately involved a recovering addict may become with his God until you first understand how far the average addict strays from God.

In writing this book, I have for emphasis' sake overstated some things and understated others. I have also changed the chronology of events from time to time, especially when talking about my own experiences. I do this not only to enliven the narrative, but to protect the lives of certain "innocent" people such as doctors, professors, and saloonkeepers.

As they say in the documentaries, the story you are about to hear is true. I can only hope it will ring true for you.

1

Taking the Pill

In the early 1960s, I was playing golf at a country club in an eastern city. On the fifth tee, I got off a good drive and found myself sprawled in the grass with an excruciating pain shooting in all directions, up, down, and sideways, from the vicinity of my lower back.

Since I happened to be playing alone that afternoon—I had planned to play only about six or seven holes before dinner—I didn't know exactly what to do. When I tried to stand, I discovered I couldn't. Not only was the pain too intense, I just couldn't stand. When I managed to get myself into the semblance of a standing position, I would fall right down again like a two-month-old baby.

I didn't want to spend the rest of the day on the fifth tee, but I couldn't see anyone nearby. I had deliberately chosen to play on a Monday so no one could watch my sloppy work on the course. So I took my golf bag handle between my teeth and crawled, like a St. Bernard dog dragging a frozen traveller, approximately one-half mile to my car.

I met only one person. He nodded pleasantly to me and asked me how I was doing. Through clenched teeth, I mumbled, "Fine." He ambled on, quite drunk, having just finished the grand golfer's ritual of winding down after eighteen arduous holes on the course in the 19th Hole Bar at the course's edge—an oasis in a desert of green.

Or maybe he hadn't played the eighteen arduous holes. Probably he was just polishing off his half pint in an outdoor setting.

As weeks went by, I really wasn't doing very well. My doctor thought I had "sciatica" and gave me a small truss which I chose to wear approximately once a week usually late at night in the bathroom after my family had gone to bed. After two months, my doctor sent me to a "bone man," as he affectionately called him, an orthopedic specialist. The bone man took some pictures of my spinal column and discovered two of my vertebrae resting suspiciously close together, suggesting that I had lost some portions of a disk. At that point I did not even know that I had disks.

Once disk cartilage "slips" from between the vertebrae, no one, including the doctor, knows quite where the thing or things have gone—unless the doctor operates. And the doctor doesn't like to do that unless the patient's pain forces him to. A depressing number of back operations don't work. So the disk or particles thereof just hang around in the lower back, prepared to touch the sciatic nerve system and electrify the whole body.

For the man or woman with a slipped or ruptured disk, death by the electric chair often seems preferable to the terrible muscle spasms and cramps, the cold sweat, the nervous tension, and the depressing realization that you'll probably never get away from this pain ever.

After I had worn a back brace and exercised my back for a month without relief, my orthopedic doctor decided to put me in traction. That is, he decided to hang some weights from my hips and immobilize me in bed for two weeks in the hospital.

Traction is one of the most ridiculous situations a human being can get himself into. Nurses frequently can't stand patients who are in traction because patients cannot stand nurses who put them in traction. Nurses must wash you, service you with bedpans and miniature urinals, scrub your back with alcohol, and convince you that you have fewer capacities than a newborn babe.

The nurses convince you that you are helpless. That is one reason why a certain type of patient receives no help whatsoever from traction. He is so mad the whole time and so tensed up over his miserable condition that his spasms make plans to get worse once he is out of the hospital.

Since back injuries produce so much pain, the patient is also likely to demand drugs to take away the pain. I did this even though I had never had a painkiller, a tranquilizer, or a sleeping pill in my life. And I was 31 at the time. My doctor gave me the drugs, and I liked them all. Soon I found a second doctor—unknown to the first doctor—who also gave me all three. I began to use the prescribed dosages given me by two doctors.

As my doctors continued to rotate me for almost a year on a dizzy merry-go-round of differing tranquilizers and barbiturates, I learned to love my doctors and the whole medical profession. The pills worked. That is one of the keys to understanding drug dependents. Drugs work!

It's simple: I had great pain. I couldn't sleep. The pills reduced my suffering. I slept like a log. I floated through every day, "coping" with my pain, working like a slaphappy beaver.

And after about three months I became a drug addict. Some of my addicted friends would say I became a dope fiend. I don't know how fiendish I became. Actually I was quite docile—a marvel to my wife, my young children, and to the members of the parish I was serving at the time. "Look," they would say, "how pastor always smiles in spite of his pain." It was true. My wife, Dottie, says I went around all the time with a goofy grin on my face, like Gomer Pyle. Of course. I was in never-never land. I was drugged all the time—on prescription pills.

So that I don't malign my doctors who did finally manage to get the pain in my back to subside, I repeat: I started after a few months to use more barbiturates than they had prescribed. And I didn't tell them about it. I needed more drugs because my body was getting used to them. I was building up that dread tolerance so dangerous for anybody taking any kind of mood-changing chemical—from alcohol to morphine. And the two doctors never discovered they were prescribing pills in tandem.

How did I get the pills? I simply went to my friendly neighborhood pharmacists and asked for refills. Two pharmacists at two drug stores. Overdosing is easy. Any intelligent patient can do it.

I emphasize that the patient does the overdosing. I think chemical dependents make a mistake trying to blame doctors and pharmacists for their own dependencies. For every doctor or pharmacist who prescribes or provides pills unwisely, there are three or four who have been tricked by their patients into prescribing unwisely. Besides, many doctors and pharmacists don't like to insult you by asking whether you're a drug addict.

13

When I went to my druggist and asked for a refill, he never asked any questions—even when I was using twice the prescribed amounts. I was a clergyman. Clergymen do not become drug addicts.

Due to recent federal legislation, pharmacists may no longer refill prescriptions for amphetamines and barbiturates with the freedom once allowed them. Doctors have been made more conscious of their responsibilities in prescribing mood-altering drugs. This is all well and good. Undoubtedly such laws will cut down on the amount of drug abuse in this country.

The laws are useful. They do not prove, however, that the fault for drug abuse lies with the professions of medicine or pharmacy. The fault lies with the drug dependent. He makes the decision to abuse—to overkill. If ever I thought I could blame a doctor or a druggist for my own difficulties with drugs—push the responsibility off on them—I might get the idea I could abuse those drugs again. If it's old Doc Welby's fault, I can exploit Doc Gannon and join the drugged fraternity once again. Marvelous idea. And quite fatal.

During my initial period of drug consumption I sometimes tried to drink. I had always liked to drink beer before I hurt my back. I usually had several bottles in the evening after meetings or conferences. To this day I don't really know whether I was drinking in an unusual pattern before the back injury or not. I do know I had lost no control over my drinking, never drank before the end of all the day's work, never even drank hard booze except at parties, and didn't know a Rhine wine from a tawny port.

That sounds funny to me now. Later I learned to chugalug a bottle of Rhine wine in sixty seconds flat.

While I was taking all those "downers" for my back, however, I didn't much care for alcohol. Without knowing anything about potentiation, the increased effects of one drug produced by the simultaneous use of a similar drug, I did notice that a bottle of beer seemed to knock me flat. I started to get frightened about becoming an alcoholic. So I abstained from alcohol and felt pious about it.

I think I knew—deep inside—that I had developed a habit for mood-changing drugs, even though I also knew I had legitimate needs for them. And I wanted, I suppose, to stay off something. I chose alcohol.

My back pain came and went, and I didn't stay off downers. Both of my doctors were delighted about the remission of my pain and withdrew my prescription privileges. I was not so delighted. I went instead to a third doctor and said I had insomnia. I did have insomnia. After using barbiturates for a solid year, I couldn't possibly go to sleep without pills. Or so it seemed. Also, though I didn't know it, I could avoid all sorts of other unpleasant effects and symptoms with those pills. Without them I could have a grand mal seizure. And break a leg or my head.

I didn't do any of those things, because my new doctor was happy to give me pills for insomnia. He had insomnia too and was very sympathetic toward people who had insomnia. Genuinely so.

"I once took barbiturates myself," he said.

For the next two years I took pills from my new doctor. When he finally began to accept the fact—I think he knew long before he accepted it—that I had become a hopeless barbiturate addict, he withdrew the prescription. And without being told, I knew this time exactly what to do. I substituted alcohol for the pills. And as every specialist in the field will tell you, alcohol substitutes perfectly well for barbiturates and tranquilizers—just as barbiturates substitute perfectly well for alcohol. I had found a solution.

The only problem was, the one drug creates a tolerance for the other in the addict's system. If you take a lot of pills to keep yourself under control, you'll take a lot of booze to accomplish the same thing. But with even worse effects.

Alcohol, you see, destroys the body like no other drug, except maybe volatile anesthetic solvents found in benzene, toluene, gasoline, and paint thinner. If you sniff too much toluene too frequently, you may do permanent damage to your brain, bone marrow, and possibly your liver and kidneys. That's terrible. But how many people sniff toluene ten times a day every day of their lives? How many people even know what toluene is? I don't. Or how many people carry around a pint of paint thinner to pull through an average day?

By contrast, everyone knows what alcohol is. And millions of people carry around their daily pints of it. Unfortunately, only a few of those millions know that alcohol may also cause permanent brain damage, liver damage, kidney damage, pancreas damage, stomach damage, heart damage, lung damage. If you can grow it, alcohol can kill it. Regular heavy drinking may even swell up your feet and make you look like you've got elephantiasis. Or produce shooting pains in your hand. Or make you think you have bamboo splinters under your fingernails.

When I turned to the grape, I was a professor of theology at one of the best-known seminaries in the country. I taught my classes and fulfilled my "duties."

But some of my close friends knew something was wrong. I was often belligerent, offensive, pushy. Or when I wasn't pushy, I was withdrawn and sulky. Though I usually taught with a considerable flair in the classroom—maybe like a half-soused John Barrymore —my students must have known I wasn't prepared, at least some of the time.

Some of my closest friends spoke to me about slowing

up intellectually. "You're not as fast as you used to be," my dearest friend said one day. "Are you depressed?"

"Yes, I'm depressed," I said happily. Happy to realize that he didn't guess I was now on Doriden.

Doriden is a sedative made from a substance called glutethimide. Many doctors believe—or used to believe —that it is a suitable substitute for barbiturates and does not form or feed drug habits very easily. I found a doctor who knew I was addicted—though he didn't exactly put it in those words—and made the decision to give me Doriden out of fear that I would have an emotional breakdown without some type of soporific drug. Also, he wanted me to stop drinking alcohol and gave me a somewhat less destructive mood-changer instead.

To this day, I value and respect his decision. He had to wait for me to discover for myself that I was addicted to downers. And then to withdraw from my drugs and confront whatever fears and obsessions had driven me to abuse the drugs in the first place. He took his chances. I took mine. He is, in my opinion, a magnificent doctor, conservative and creative, as all good doctors must be. As I was to discover, the element of risk is always present in the treatment of drug dependency.

So, I was back on pills and off alcohol. Doriden has some advantages over alcohol. It does not attack your body like Genghis Khan. Doriden does not make your breath smell.

When abused, however, it does make you walk with a slight tilt. In fact, on large doses of Doriden, the body walks into walls instead of through doors. And falls over desks rather than steps around them. And occasionally falls off chairs during the family dinner hour. Or best yet, the body falls out of the bathtub and onto the bathroom floor.

I slept one night with my head pillowed against the toilet bowl. Like Jacob sleeping on a rock at Bethel.

17

Jacob, however, woke up with visions of angels moving to and from heaven. I woke up with a brilliantly clear view of the water line showing coldly quiet against the white porcelain of the toilet bowl. A horrifying and humiliating experience.

I took so many Doriden tablets per average day that I finally had to go into the local hospital for a rest cure— of three days. That meant my doctor stopped giving me Doriden and fed me gallons of orange juice. For two days I was quite happy, basking like a baby in an Anita Bryant commercial. On the third day, however, I did not rise. I got jittery instead. The third night I didn't sleep. I lay awake staring at the 100-watt light bulb over my head. On the fourth day I was released. Cured.

I was also diarrhetic, spastic, paranoid, and visionary. Everywhere I looked I saw light bulbs. When my doctor came in to give me his blessing, I thought he had been transfigured. He was encompassed by a halo of GE soft light.

I did not express my gratitude to him, however. I thought he was trying to kill me. He was—for my own good. I had once again proved myself to be irresponsible with mood-changing drugs. The doctor had to take me off Doriden.

But that can be dangerous too. With the peculiar authority nurtured by desperation, I demanded drugs for my newly developing disease: palsy. Though he seemed unwilling to talk about my palsy, he sent me home with a prescription for a minor tranquilizer, good for any occasion and condition.

Minor tranquilizers had never done much for me. I must have a hardy constitution and fantastic tolerance for mood-changers. I have seen people fairly balmy on Librium. All I ever got was sluggish and irregular—in need of Haley's M-O. And developing a passion for

Haley's M-O is difficult even for a panic-stricken drug addict.

When I got home I took no Librium. Sick unto death I took a tumbler of bourbon, and cured myself.

Dottie and my two kids, twelve and ten years old, could not believe, however, that I was cured. They said, in chorus, "You're drunk!" And they were right.

My dear Dottie wheeled me flat on my back into the hospital, full of Doriden. Four days later I lay flat on my back in our bedroom, full of Old Crow.

I wasn't cured. That, in fact, was the beginning of a necessary end for me. I kept on drinking day after day for about two months. My doctor now wouldn't give me any more pills containing a sufficient wallop to keep my nervous system even in a state of functioning disorder. He stood by with me waiting for my decision to ask for help. Frantically I tried across-the-counter (the pharmacologists call them "proprietary") sleeping pills. They made me peptic and took away my last shred of good humor. The only thing that worked was dear ethyl alcohol.

Why do drug dependents take their drugs? Because they work. That's at least part of the answer. Like prayer, drugs change things. Alcohol cures palsy caused by withdrawal from barbiturates. It also produces seven other diseases worse than the first. It keeps on changing things until you don't recognize your own face in the mirror.

I began my experiment with alcohol. It turned out to be a short experiment.

2

Taking the Plunge

With alcohol I entered my period of The Great Change.

Because I wanted to convince myself I wasn't spending too much money on booze, I drank A & P Rhine wine at less than a dollar a fifth. The only trouble was, I usually drank four or five bottles a day. I suppose I did save some money, but I kept myself in a state of suspended animation, of perpetual glow.

This part of my experience I cannot really fathom, and no drug addict, I suspect, ever does, fully. I knew by now I was hooked, dependent, addicted, alcoholic, everything. I couldn't pretend to myself that I was merely a drug addict and not an alcoholic. I couldn't pretend to myself that I was merely an alcoholic and not a drug addict. I was everything.

I figured God could help me somehow, and everyday begged or demanded relief from him. But both my pleas and my demands amounted to pure mockery, because I didn't really believe God would do anything constructive for me. Or more importantly, *I didn't want*

God to do anything which might jeopardize my dependency on drugs.

I couldn't imagine a life without my drugs. So I neatly substituted my drugs for the God I had once depended on.

God did not fail *me* in my most miserable hour. I simply made it impossible for *him* to reach me—at least with his grace. I knew he was there, even if I didn't recognize him. I felt this judgment in everything I did. He hemmed me in with his power, while day by day I became more and more powerless. But I continued to look elsewhere for help.

For instance, I read everything about drugs I could get my hands on. I read Ginsberg's *Howl* and Burrough's *Naked Lunch* and discovered I was a mere novitiate in the fraternity of the drugged. I read Jackson's *The Lost Weekend* and discovered I had at least passed initiation. I read Dr. Harold T. Hyman's *The Complete Home Medical Encyclopedia* and discovered that I was a "sot" "beclouding and ruining the lives of the immediate household." And the lives of my doctors who were going through an "ordeal" with me.

"Sooner or later," wrote Dr. Hyman, the doctor becomes "discouraged, disgusted and thoroughly disheartened." I felt particularly guilty about that. I felt guilty about the "ordeal" good old Doc Hyman went through just writing his little section on "Alcohol and Alcoholism." And I'd never even met Dr. Hyman who had sold over 400,000 copies of his home medical encyclopedia, says Avon, his publisher.

Spurred on by Dr. Hyman, I began for the first time to seek the company of my fellow sots. But I was a total failure. I could not make a friend of a single sot. I went to small, intimate, high-priced bars at the cocktail hour and watched happy sots swallowing Chivas Regal or

Beefeaters by the hour. But I could never manage a successful conversation, let alone a sottish friendship.

I once came close in a bar frequented by the town's newspaper reporters. When I told them I had a degree in English, they occasionally asked me questions about split infinitives and the use of *whom* and *who*. But they were unhappy with my conservative answers and talked derisively about the halls of academe. When the bartender started calling me "the professor," I took my besotten trade elsewhere.

I tried a small bar with a large sign saying BUDWEISER in huge print and BONNY'S AND AL'S in a fine line beneath the BUDWEISER. Bonny worked the bar. I never met Al.

BUDWEISER, BONNY'S AND AL'S was full of moody sots swallowing shots of Ancient Age and bottles of Busch beer by the hours. They never asked me questions about anything. Mostly they sat hunched between their bottles, growling about their wives, the President, the St. Louis Cardinals, and assorted people whose heads they would like to bash in. Actually, they talked only about the latter since the heads of their wives, the President, and the St. Louis Cardinals were high on the list to be bashed.

I once struck up a conversation by asking why anyone should want to bash in the heads of the St. Louis Cardinals since they were winning the pennant for the second year in a row. One of my companions at the bar looked at me carefully and asked, "Are you a detective?" I was so startled I said, "Yes." "I thought so," he said, and left me to myself.

The next and the last time I went to BUDWEISER, BONNY'S AND AL'S, I asked the same man why he thought I was a detective. "I can tell by your eyes," he said, and left me to myself again.

This is what the experts call "seeking companions on lower social levels." It is a red-flag symptom of chronic alcoholism or drug dependency. It also didn't work for me. If you look like a detective, you can't successfully find lower companions in places like BUDWEISER, BONNY'S AND AL'S. In my opinion, I could have devoted two months to the project and still have failed to find a single lower companion. I couldn't even throw darts or play miniature shuffleboard. Lower companions maintain their own standards. I couldn't meet them.

So I returned to "isolated drinking" at home. Drinking by yourself and drinking with lower companions, by the way, are both common symptoms of chronic drug addiction.

I drank morning, noon, night, and dropped off in a mild coma. Each night before dropping off, I knew I would stop the next day. This couldn't go on, obviously. Each morning I went out and bought two more bottles of A & P Rhine wine. I could go on.

I had the craziest excuses for buying Rhine wine at 9:00 A.M. I talked to more check-out girls about more friends, more relatives, more business associates, more mothers and mothers-in-law who had just dropped in and couldn't get by a day without Rhine wine. I pretended to be eating more fish and fowl which demanded just the right touch of Rhine wine, A & P brand at 89¢. Nothing against A & P. A & P was a godsend.

Dottie went to work at 8:00, and I taught classes. That last semester I had classes at 11:00 A.M. and 1:00 P.M. I would down an entire bottle of Rhine wine in minutes at 9:00 to get an instant effect. And everything would seem all right. I would then prepare my classes. By 11:00 the wine had begun to wear off, and I would get through the class. I would then hang on through my 1:00 class and drink the second bottle at 2:05 P.M., always rushing home with ready excuses for all students who wanted to stay in the classroom and talk— or ask questions about assignments or grades.

Always I was in a hurry. I had to say hello to those relatives, friends, acquaintances, professional colleagues by the legions whom I hadn't seen for years, or mothers and mothers-in-law staying at my house. My students must have thought I ran a hotel.

The end came when I discovered one bottle at 9:00 wasn't enough. I finished one at 9:00 and the second at 9:06. I reasoned that if I got them down fast, I could throw them both off by 11:00. I discovered I couldn't. I came to class late and meandered through my lecture, talking about the flu. I had the flu all right. Then I felt so guilty when I finished the class, I ran back to the A & P and bought a third bottle and had it at 12:05. This was the first time I didn't meet a class.

The next day I didn't meet either of my classes. I called my secretary at 9:00 A.M. to let my first class know I had pleurisy. I forgot to tell my second class anything. By 4:30 P.M. when my wife and kids got home from work and school, I had downed about five bottles of Rhine wine and four or five martinis at a little bar next to our local A & P.

I never drank in our neighborhood bars because clergy who are professors at seminaries take chances when they drink in their friendly neighborhood establishments. People frown on drinking clergymen more readily than they frown on drinking mothers with small babes in arms. Even students become mildly derisive.

That afternoon I took my chances. To this day I couldn't tell you whether anyone was in the bar at all. Who knows? Maybe I finally made a friend from the lower classes and can't even remember him.

Without knowing it clearly, I had given up in my struggles against my panoply of mood-changers. When Dottie came through the door, I said—and I remember *this* as clear as a bell despite all the booze—"I missed my classes today. This is it!" And I remember being angry when she said, "So what's so bad about missing classes?"

I had forgotten that she had wheeled me in and out of a hospital flat on my back. She had seen me higher than a kite hundreds of times. She had seen me "miss" everything imaginable. But I had never missed an important job assignment—goofed off horribly, but never missed.

Now I had missed a specific obligation of high order. A class. That's what I meant. Given my kind of soul, I couldn't go on doing that. That *was* it. But I knew tomorrow I would do the same thing. And knew I could not go on doing the same thing.

That night I sobered up a little, and told my wife I had to go into a hospital for the treatment of—I didn't even know what to call it. I called it drug addiction. And I was right. I was a multiple-drug dependent. I had developed dependencies and cross-tolerance upon alcohol, barbiturates, synthetic soporifics, and minor tranquilizers.

Dottie and I talked until about 1:00 A.M. We knew where I had to go. A group of sober alcoholics with means who had themselves received treatment for drug dependency, and non-alcoholics who knew others who had received treatment, had recently established in our city a foundation for the prevention and treatment of such disorders. As their first accomplishment, they had hired an expert director who had staffed a private hospital devoted exclusively to the treatment of alcoholism and related drug dependencies. The treatment philosophy was closely modeled on that of Hazelden center in Center City, Minnesota.

I knew one of the men who had received treatment at Hazelden and helped to establish our local hospital. My wife and I decided I would talk the next day to the president of my seminary, tell him the facts about my illness, share my decision with a few close colleagues, and with my doctor, call my friend and go into the hospital.

The next morning I didn't want to do any of those things. I wanted to go to the A & P and get my 89¢ bottles of Rhine wine. I wanted to teach my classes. I wanted to get back into harness after just one more day of drinking. But Dottie held firm, and actually so did I.

That night I talked to my school president. He had not guessed that I was addicted to drugs. He and my closest friends realized that I was experiencing some kind of problem. He was both happy and relieved to discover that I knew what the problem was and that Dottie and I knew what I should do about it. He chose to support me, and immediately offered me an indefinite leave of absence. Someone else would take my classes. I would meet with them one more time and tell them I was going into the hospital.

Those classes were the hardest I ever taught in my life. I wanted to tell my students what I was doing and why, and I didn't. I ended up saying that I was going into the hospital for a checkup.

It turned out to be one of the longest checkups on record. Five and one-half weeks. It was the worst five weeks—and in some respects the best—I ever spent in my life.

Siegfried Reinhardt 1975.

3

In Treatment–
Hitting Bottom

The moment I got into the hospital, I decided I didn't want to be there. I began making a fool of myself every chance I got. I also acted, as my counselor, my head nurse, and my fellow patients later told me, like a prima donna.

Doctors, lawyers, professors, and clergymen in treatment for drug disorders often act like prima donnas because they think they're superior to everyone in the hospital, including counselors and medical staff. Most addicts in treatment try to hold on to their false pride as long as they can. If you have a lot of misbegotten pride in yourself and your magnificent achievements in life, you take a long time losing it. But lose it you must.

The first step of the program of Alcoholics Anonymous reads: "We admitted we were powerless over alcohol—that our lives had become unmanageable." The staff of the hospital I entered believed no drug dependent could find a sober and satisfying way of life unless he accepted the reality of A.A.'s Step One for his life.

I resisted the step.

When Eileen, the head nurse, attempted to put me through an admissions interview. I told her I belonged behind her desk and she belonged in my chair.

"I should be doing the interviewing," I said, bursting with manly pride, and falling off my chair from the pint of gin I had consumed just before walking through the hospital doors.

I also decided I needed a private room. I had nothing against drunks and addicts in general. In person, however, they could be embarrassing. I didn't get my private room. The hospital staff believed addicts recovered best in close company with other addicts.

It took me some time to admit to myself that I was even in a hospital for the treatment of alcoholism and related disorders. Even there within the hospital walls, I tried to deny the plain reality of my predicament.

I pretended, for instance, that I was doing research on drug addiction. I was going to write a definitive treatise on the subject. Or I pretended I was out slumming, just passing through the neighborhood.

As the days wore on, however, the truth began to sink in. Slowly.

I discovered, for one thing, that everyone on the staff, doctors, counselors, nurses, social workers, priests, dietitians, maintenance engineers, and the charwoman, kept me under constant surveillance, as if I were a criminal suspect. The staff members talked with me, or watched me amble around the premises, chatting here and chatting there, and then they made little notes about me in my file at the nurses' station. Everyone, I thought, is writing my community biography. I didn't realize at first that all of those people were writing all of those things down for my own good. If the staff members didn't write out their observations of my peculiar behavior, they might forget everything about me—which, at that point, would have been just fine with me.

Now, as a member of a hospital staff treating alcoholics, I myself sometimes write down notes about patients' behavior. But just occasionally I still find it sneaky. It makes the patient feel exposed, like a naked jaybird in hell—a necessary stage, unfortunately, in the treatment for drug addiction.

For years I tried to cover up my addiction. Now everyone around me had to uncover my secret at my expense.

With the illness of chemical dependency, the way up to relief is the way down to miserable suffering. The addict cannot experience the heavenly joys of freedom from his drugs unless he first inhabits the depths of hell and recognizes where he is. The necessity of plummeting the depths is one of the hardest truths to digest for any drug dependent, especially for a proud one like myself.

Plummeting the depths may sound romantic. Actually it's very messy. For everyone: for the long-suffering patient, for the long-suffering members of his family, and for the long-suffering treatment team. Everyone suffers on the way to recovery. If later I sound like a broken record repeating this refrain, I hope you will realize why. No one on God's earth wants to suffer at all. But every alcoholic and drug dependent must suffer miserably if he expects to begin a new life without his drugs.

During the first three or four days of my treatment, the doctors and nurses gave me minor tranquilizers to allow my nerves to settle into some facsimile of law and order. Once I seemed in reasonably good physical health and not about to curl up in a depressed fetal position behind the trash can in the laundry room, the staff took me off mood-changing drugs altogether.

For the first time in seven years or so, I began to exist without any chemical substance designed to send me into the land of Nod. I went "cold turkey."

The phrase, cold turkey, comes from the gooseflesh experienced by a drug addict withdrawing from heroin. I have never had any heroin, so I can't speak with personal authority of the particular gooseflesh produced by withdrawal from that deadly drug. The phrase, however, will apply very well to withdrawal from alcohol, barbiturates, and especially to those two drugs in combination.

In withdrawal from barbiturates and alcohol, you feel and sometimes look like a cold turkey. Not only do you get goose flesh, you feel like a plucked goose—all shriveled up, physically, emotionally, and spiritually. And the fact that every organ in your body starts acting as if it had a life of its own doesn't help one bit.

For a short period in withdrawal, you feel completely out of control. You were out of control drinking and popping pills too, but you didn't think so. And until the bottom fell out, you didn't feel that way either. With a good glow on, you thought grandly, "I am the king of all that I survey." Now you feel like a kook. All the world is surveying you and writing a book about you.

And your multiple muscle spasms (what drunks like to call "the shakes"), diarrhea, upper and lower back pains, migraines in both your head and feet, spastic colon, strangulating esophagus, jumping eyeballs, and your over-powering urge to kill someone—mostly yourself—do little to convince you otherwise.

After a few days in total withdrawal, your body doesn't complain that much anymore. But your mind keeps chanting familiar refrains. "I'm going crazy," it says. "I'll get the shakes and spill hot coffee on my groin," it says. So you do get the shakes and spill hot coffee on your groin, which produces another worry.

"You're impotent," your mind says to you. "You'll return to normal society a eunuch with the palsy."

You may be able to face your fellow patients, some

of whom are shaking as badly as you are and also have scalded groins. But you can't face your wife in this condition. Or if she's a saintly and self-sacrificial type, you know you'll never face your best friends and your seminary president, and your students who think you're in the hospital for a routine five-week checkup for high blood pressure.

How can you write on the blackboard with your hand performing like a flea circus? The mind's a busy bee during treatment for alcoholism.

Again, there's little point in getting romantic about all of this. Withdrawal symptoms are the least of your worries in treatment, unless they happen to kill you. And with a good treatment team, you're not likely to die in withdrawal from anything you've been ingesting, from Old Crow through Seconol. Or even Aqua Velva and vanilla extract.

A skillful staff brings you along gradually until your body and soul have regained some semblance of equilibrium. Body and soul, in fact, begin to rediscover each other in the same person. And you begin to discover that you can get out of this mess, maybe.

You're still a long way from home. You need a great deal of counsel, and so you get a counselor.

Already during my withdrawal period, I acquired a counselor who began to convince me that I'd made a total catastrophe of my life. I didn't expect this.

I had been to several other hospitals to dry out from pills and alcohol. There the staff fed me orange juice, checked my vital symptoms, made minimal notes in my files, and said such things as, "How are you feeling today, Duane?"

I always said, "Fine," grinning through the purple grog patches on my face.

One day a nurse said, "Duane, you're looking much

better today," and I felt like a new man, hale and hearty, unconsciously preparing to dive back into the bottle the moment they let me off the ward.

A resident internist told me, "If you don't stop drinking and taking so many pills, you're going to die, Reverend Mehl," but I expected this from my kindly young internist, who was treating me for tired blood or colitis or retarded depression, or something equally superficial to cover for my miserable alcoholic condition.

After several days everyone said with a bright smile, "Duane, you're looking one-hundred percent better." And I, like a fool, thought they were right. So when they let me out of the hospital, I promptly celebrated my one-hundred percent improvement with a festive tumbler of Old Crow. Usually I waited for a couple of weeks or maybe a month. But I got back to my drugs quickly enough.

In the last hospital I entered, however, my counselor, Frank, said, "Duane, you look terrible, and for the next week or so we're going to discover things that will make you look and feel twice as bad as you look and feel now."

I'll never forget my counselor saying to me: "Start thinking about how powerless you are over alcohol and how unmanageable your life has become and write about it on paper so you won't forget it. And by the way," he said, "you'll probably get depressed doing all this. Don't worry. Everybody gets depressed."

"Don't worry," he said. That's the basic reason I took all those downers all those years. I was worried. I thought I'd get depressed without drugs, get irrational, go crazy, and do something silly and fatal. "Now," Frank says, "you'll get depressed, so don't worry."

I did get depressed and at first I worried about it morning, noon, and night.

My counselor also gave me a test to prove to me beyond the shadow of a doubt that I was a chronic drug addict, dependent both on alcohol and on barbiturates. Of the twenty-or-so questions, I failed about eighteen. I had done everything from drink in the morning and hide bottles, to deteriorate socially, morally, and spiritually in relationship to God, man, and beast.

Frank also told me that Dottie would have to take the same test. "But Dottie hardly even drinks," I said with indignation. "You don't understand," Frank said. "She'll answer the same questions *about you.* That way we can compare your view of yourself with her view and see who's the most reliable."

The scheme must have driven me to rigid honesty. I can yet remember, with sweet joy, that Dottie and I answered the form exactly the same way. Actually, I had stopped trying to deceive her several years before I entered intensive treatment, for which I thank God. Our honesty with one another helped to keep us close, despite my sickening behavior.

As I began to meditate on my powerlessness over alcohol and my unmanageable life, I entered the first phrase of my treatment for drug dependency. Physical withdrawal from my drugs was a mere passing annoyance compared with the emotional and spiritual anguish I experienced during my assessment of the quagmire my life had become.

Since I have always been able to write with a fair sense of ease and satisfaction, I found a typewriter in the hospital and began writing about my inability as an addict to manage my life. The more I wrote, the more I realized that I had little ability to manage my life before or after I became an addict. I began to sink into the quicksand of my past sins and suddenly obvious shortcomings.

I began remembering and accepting responsibility for things in my past so silly and so degrading they made my hands rattle on the typewriter keys when I wrote about them.

I remembered the time my family and I had gone on vacation to a motel on a lake in the Ozarks. On the trip down I popped pills and Dottie did the driving. On arriving I stepped out of the car and promptly fell asleep in the middle of the motel owner's petunia bed. Mumbling something about sleeping sickness, Dottie and my two kids, Jenny and Dave, dragged me bodily into our room. The next day mortified and sick unto death, we drove home with one day of vacation under our belts.

My family went nowhere else that summer. Shakingly, I wrote it all down under the heading *Selfishness*.

I remembered the time we were eating dinner and I was high on Rhine wine. Jenny and Dave were mimicking my elaborately careful ritual of steering food from the immense distance of plate to mouth. In a flash I became furious at them and pushed at the table. Dottie, sitting quietly on a chair at the other end of the table, suddenly found herself lying on her back on the floor with a bowl of mashed potatoes in the middle of her chest. Jenny and David began yelling, and I started chattering about reserves of physical strength I didn't even know I possessed. I flexed my muscles, hoping they would find me humorous.

They didn't stay to catch my act. They went out to eat at MacDonalds, and left me to meditate on the mashed potatoes. I wrote it all down under the heading *"Thoughtlessness."*

I remembered the time I walked off the end of my patio at a party, breaking the fifth metatarsal bone in my left foot. I simply stepped off, laughingly, into the void, spilling my tumbler of bourbon down my shirt front.

I was so embarrassed I said nothing to my friends about the piercing pain in my foot. Nine days later, hobbling around on homemade crutches, I still talked vaguely about a sprained ankle. When I finally went to the doctor, he told me I had set a new time record for continuing to function on a broken foot, a record for stupidity and self-deception.

I wrote it all down under the heading *Miscellaneous.*

Step One is an excruciating experience for yourself and for your counselor. He must encourage you and guide you in the exposure of the truth about your disordered behavior under the influence of drugs. On the other hand, he must maintain empathy with you all the way down to the bottom.

A counselor trained to treat alcoholic and related addicts must be a hardy soul. Frequently he is an alcoholic himself, dry for some years and free from pills, devoting his life to others who have the same illness. But now he must tell one patient after another, "You've created a catastrophe for a life. You're responsible for this mess. You're going to go through hell accepting that responsibility. But try to be honest about your life and let's see what happens."

The counselor doesn't know exactly what's going to happen. Neither do you, the patient. You may come out of your depression, and you may not. You do begin to grasp one fact: you and you alone must accept both the reality of your illness and your responsibility for it before you have any chance for a recovering process. You must furthermore accept the reality that *you, by yourself, possess no power to extricate yourself from your predicament!*

I mean this quite literally. In phase one of treatment, I came to both realizations almost simultaneously. I had to bear the fundamental responsibility for my state of being. By myself I could do nothing to change my state of being.

When you compress those two realizations into one,

37

you begin to understand why so many people in the first step of treatment for chemical dependency have an excruciating time of it.

I didn't sleep for five days or nights. After five nights without sleep, you get edgy, irritable, low. You feel as if you've just taken henbane and found out it isn't working.

A friend of mine found herself so depressed and angry during the first phase of treatment that she started writing nasty letters to everyone she knew. Fortunately, her friends saved the letters and gave them back to her later for her scrapbook. That scrapbook is a montage encapsulating the step one experience for many drug dependents in hospital treatment.

In one letter she compared herself with a catatonic, three-toed sloth. She'd slowed down a bit.

In another, she compared herself with a manic cheetah. She'd sped up a bit.

In another, she compared herself with Bela Lugosi. She wanted to suck blood from her counselor's neck, and not purely for the sake of nourishment.

In a fourth letter, she was the prisoner in Edgar Allen Poe's "The Pit and the Pendulum." One difference: she dropped down the hole.

Step one for more recovering alcoholics and drug addicts *is* something like dropping down a hole. The founders of A.A. were brilliantly accurate in their description of recovery from alcoholism. There is no way up from addiction to mood-changing drugs without moving down to full acceptance of the horrible helplessness of addiction. And unless the addict accepts his powerlessness over his drug, and his inability to manage his life, he has no chance for recovery.

Many of us who pass through step one in an A.A. fellowship or in a treatment center actually undergo an experience of total powerlessness on a particular date at a particular moment.

Mine came late at night as I tried unsuccessfully to fall asleep. My roommate snored, and airplanes roared overhead for takeoffs and landings at a nearby airport. I was feeling mildly sorry for myself when suddenly I experienced—not realized, but experienced in my body and my mind—my own responsibility for my condition in life. Everything I had been thinking about and writing down on paper came crashing in on me like tons of sand, surrounding every limb of my body, smothering my face, and pouring in torrents through my brain.

All at once I felt I was the worst human being ever born. Not simply an average, run-of-the-mill, frail, but charming man. Not simply as bad as the worst friend, acquaintance, or enemy I could think of, but worse than anybody else on God's green earth.

I remember calculating the man I disliked the most in life, and came up with a brute I'll call Bruce. I thought about his utterly selfish manner of dominating every conversation, of his utterly vulgar habits of speech, of his tendency to attack every person he talked about, always finding them "beneath contempt," of his open brutality toward his wife—and I found myself a mile ahead of him in faults and shortcomings.

The feeling was catastrophic. It persisted through much of the night. After dozing slightly and eating breakfast, I shared my experience with Frank, my counselor. I said, "I feel as if I'm riding on a roller coaster out of control. I have no power to produce any change whatsoever."

And Frank leaned back in his chair and said, "Good, I think you just took step one. Bring it up in your group this afternoon."

In phase one of treatment, every bad experience is

potentially a good experience. And every experience, good and bad, seems a commonplace to staff members and to those fellow patients who have progressed a little further in their recovery than you have.

I shared my feelings with my group in therapy session that afternoon, and sure enough: no one in my circle seemed astonished or even mildly surprised to hear about them. Rather, most members of the group seemed pleased. A few people nodded sagely, as if I were their guru and had just uttered something quite profound.

One man said that same thing happened to him at the breakfast table about a week before. Another said he had gone forty days and forty nights, or some such period, without sleep before he finally knew that his life was unmanageable. The counselor in our group described an experience very similar to mine. He said he woke up one night, while in treatment, and felt in a kind of waking nightmare that he was hanging by his fingertips from a cliff. Suddenly he let go and fell into the void. "That was the moment," the counselor said, "when I experienced utter powerlessness over alcohol and over every other aspect of my life."

He didn't know where he was going to land. I didn't know whether I would ever get out from under the tons of sand covering my body and soul. You feel as if you may land and get out in heaven. You feel you may land and get out in hell. For a while you're just not sure which it will be.

In a treatment community, however, the addict drops into the void in the company of his counselor, his fellow patients, and other members of his treatment team. That is the critically important difference between trying to sober up on your own—muscling it like old Charles Atlas—and sobering up through a treatment program.

The counselors, the doctors, nurses, social workers,

clergy, cooks, handymen, and fellow recovering patients really do stand with you and help you on the way down to acceptance of your powerlessness—and hopefully on the way up to acceptance of powers greater than you could ever muster for your recovery.

4

In Treatment—
Climbing Out of a Hole

When a patient in a treatment facility of the type I
entered has experienced step one in recovery, his counselor then begins to talk to him about steps two and
three. Steps two and three of recovery in my hospital
again resembled very closely the description of recovery
from alcoholism in the second and third steps of the A.A.
program.

Step Two of the program reads: "Came to believe that
a power greater than ourselves could restore us to sanity."

Step Three reads: "Made a decision to turn our will
and our lives over to the care of God as we understand
Him."

The steps obviously place a heavy emphasis on God
and his involvement in the drug addict's life. That
emphasis prevents many addicts from attempting to experience these steps at all. For a while I was no excep-
tion. I felt particularly queasy about those steps because
I was a clergyman, and I felt that people expected me
to breeze right through them. Actually, I didn't have the
vaguest idea how to make a start.

Very few alcoholics or drug dependents come into hospital treatment or into A.A. meetings feeling acutely religious. If we once had a close relationship with God, we now have a close relationship with our drugs. And we can't serve two masters. Both God and drugs are jealous powers. We can't play games with one or the other.

I entered treatment a practicing atheist, or at least an agnostic. I feared, loved, and trusted my drugs above all things. After two weeks in treatment, however, I realized I needed God or some power greater than myself to take the place of my disappearing drugs. And what should I do about it?

I began by doing all the wrong things.

Mostly I tried to conjure up God in a box or a bottle. I wanted a rescuing genie.

I prayed self-conscious prayers, pouring abuse on myself in verbal torments and begging for God's mercy, and got nothing in return but a sense of my own flair for masochistic rhetoric.

I reminded God of my humility, and of his obligation to show mercy to me. I waited around and got nothing at all for my helpful reminders.

I gave God time limits to make his response to my prayers. "By the end of the week," I said, "I expect to believe in thy power to restore me to health so that I can make a decision to turn my life and will over to thee," and felt pleased as punch about the latitude I allowed God. The end of the week rolled around, and I had no power to restore myself to health and made no decisions to turn my life over to God.

Obviously, I tried to do the whole thing myself. And when you're working with God over any sort of problem in your life, you just can't manipulate him to your convenience, even if you think you've dropped into the Black Hole of Calcutta.

God must wait for you to let down your guard, humbly, so that he can catch you unawares. He must surprise you with his grace. Then you realize it has come entirely from him. And you can stop going through the agony of playing God to yourself.

My moment of grace in the hospital came after I listened one Friday afternoon to a lecture delivered by a Roman Catholic priest who served on the hospital staff. The priest talked several times each week, and I had previously paid little attention to him. In fact, since we were in the same profession I usually sat in my chair and smirked at him on account of his theological incompetencies.

During the first few weeks I smirked at all the lecturers at the hospital for their incompetencies, even when they spoke brilliantly about aspects of alcoholism and drug addiction I had never heard of. I disliked the role of a student. I was a teacher, I thought, and belonged behind the podium, not among the desks.

On this Friday afternoon, the priest spoke about the popular A.A. saying, "Let Go, Let God," which had always struck me as particularly corny. Between affected yawns I heard him say: "When you experience step two, you let go of your pride and God takes you into his hands. All you do is let go," he said. "God takes it from there."

The idea buzzed in the back of my brain through the day and into the evening. It continued to buzz there when I tried to say my prayers that night.

The staff at the hospital encouraged us to begin a regular prayer schedule centering on our difficulties with drugs. I had made a bare beginning with wooden and self-conscious petitions, full of thees and thous, and reeking with self-pity. "Dear God, thou Almighty Redeemer," I kept saying in one way or another, "please help me because I'm suffering so much." I thought I

45

was the world's champion sufferer and deserved some kind of prize from the judge of such contests.

That night I went to sleep without praying. I simply concentrated on doing nothing, relaxing beneath that ton weight of guilt and pain I was feeling. I can do nothing about it myself, I said, and fell asleep.

When I woke the next morning, curiously refreshed, I felt little or no weight on my chest or my soul. I got up with the conscious thought in my mind: Let God have my day; I'll tag along with him.

All through the day the thought persisted in my mind: It's God's day. I must accept whatever happens during his day.

I do not believe I fully turned my will or life over to God while I was in the hospital. But I made the necessary start. Day after day I realized that time belonged to God. I had to depend on his resources, his power and grace, to find my way through his day.

That was the sum and substance of what the A.A. program would call my initial "spiritual awakening" from the torpor of addiction. I wasn't blinded into a conversion experience on any road to Damascus. My awakening was quiet and unspectacular. But for that moment it sufficed. As Frank, my counselor, told me one day: "You turned your life over to *someone* other than yourself." I had done just that.

In part I had given my life over to the care and counsel of my treatment team and to the whole community of people in the hospital. I put my need for sobriety in their hands and received powers for sober survival from them in return. I had begun also to turn my life over to God—though I yet kept him at a considerable distance, as I was later to learn. I am a proud person, and God made demands on me which did not quite fit my lifestyle and schedule.

In my treatment program at the hospital, however,

I had finally reached the confession stage of recovery.

When a patient had ruminated for some weeks about his unmanageable life, and had begun to find powers outside of himself for new management of that life, he was required by his counselor to go through an experience remarkably like private confession. Even to a Protestant like myself, who'd never been in a confessional booth, it seemed remarkably like private confession.

Frank suggested that I take stock of myself again and in two or three days write down an "inventory" of my life—of my liabilities and my assets, my past failures and my hopes for the future. He gave me a pamphlet to help me out with the procedure. When I was finished, I would read my statement to a pastor on the staff.

For an alcoholic this is a sobering thought. He has in his drinking career developed so many "character defects"—as they quaintly call them in A.A.—and has created so many family, social, business, and community disasters, that writing an inventory of the mess and talking about it with some strange cleric seems like an invitation to write his own obituary without benefit of dying.

Since I had already made a running start in step one by writing down random memories of my past behavior, I practically wrote a book for my inventory. I produced fifteen pages under the category *Selfishness* alone.

Again, I have to resist the temptation of becoming romantic about this stage of treatment. It is possible even now for me to brag about the past "selfish" actions. Recovering alcoholics often do it, especially when they get caught up in a drunkologue, a picaresque and usually exaggerated narrative of their wicked wiles and ways of the past. Other alcoholics who must listen often wish they'd start drinking and stop talking.

Sometimes, the narrator of a drunkologue is about to

have another drink, or has already swallowed it down. Like a man back from armed combat, he finds civilian life a hopeless bore. He still wants to be the life of the party, even when no party is going on. He thinks everyone must be interested in his drunken past.

But if you're honest with yourself and write down your inventory seriously, you discover that your past selfish actions are neither wildly interesting nor even romantically whimsical.

When you knocked all the food off the table at dinner that night, you did not act adventuresomely. You acted like a barbarian.

When you drank up half the grocery budget every month of the year, you did not behave charmingly like Robin Hood, but irresponsibly like Jack the Ripper. You might just as well have stolen money from your wife's pocketbook, or your children's piggy banks. In fact, you did, and you remember it.

By our present social standards, you deserve to be in jail, just as surely as any junkie who steals your color TV set to buy his next fix on the streets. Your family should have hauled you down to the local sheriff.

When you worked at ten or twenty percent capacity, giving half-baked lectures to your students, unintelligible reports at your department meetings (if you went at all), always hung over with the stark-raving shakes and horrors, or mulling along in the land of Nod, you were not helpful to anyone except a few students studying to become specialists in the field of drug addiction. They may have used you as a walking—or stumbling—case study. To everyone else, you were nothing less than a goldbrick. They should have fired you.

The point needs hammering home. All sorts of people should have stranded you, left you, arrested you, fired you, and if—as in my case—they didn't, you have reason only to give thanks to them, and to God, but for God's sake, make no bones about your selfish actions toward everyone involved.

Because you have been selfish and harmful toward so many people, you must in clear and simple language express what you have done in and with your life. In concrete English words. No vague confessions of occasional selfishness or perhaps a stray outburst of nasty temper. You must make confessions of real and miserably selfish and hostile acts toward real people you really made miserable.

You don't write: I. Tendency Toward Loss of Temper, and move on to II. You write:

I. Brutality

   A. Family

      1. Knocking my wife against the kitchen stove with the front burners on, or whatever best illustrates *your* brutality toward *your* family members. And then you move on to A.2. and A.3., to brutal acts against friends and fellow employees, and so forth.

When I completed this procedure, I spoke as clearly and as simply as possible about my discoveries to a pastor on the hospital staff. He listened carefully, asked a few questions, and dismissed me with his blessing. If I had wished for absolution, I'm sure he would have absolved me. At this point in my treatment program I still wasn't feeling *that religious.*

The process incorporates steps four and five of the A.A. program. It provides the alcoholic and drug dependent the chance finally to unload his feelings of guilt in the presence of a stern but empathic person. If the alcoholic goes through the discipline seriously, he will experience a sense of relief not unlike the reprieve received by a prisoner on death row.

Young people in the 1960s developed a useful phrase for describing cathartic revelations of personal problems and needs: letting it all hang out. In phases four and five of treatment in my hospital, the patient lets it all hang out so that he can begin to get it all together again.

The experience is difficult to describe and may be one of the glories reserved for drug dependents alone. Later I want to draw some parallels between recovery from drug addiction and recovery from other kinds of spiritual malaise and malady. For now, I can only say that the feeling of relief from addiction can be so beautiful that afterwards it seems almost worth all the horror that went into its preparation. I don't really mean that, but it seemed that way to me afterwards.

I began to discover, for instance, that people still respected me and loved me simply for what I nakedly was. As I neared the conclusion of my hospital treatment, Dottie seemed happy just to see me walking with two legs on the ground rather than on thin air or through walls. When someone seems happy just to see you walking, you know she must somehow love you.

When your kids seem happy just to see you sitting rather than falling out of your chair, you know what you had probably forgotten for years: people do love you. In the back of your mind the idea is brewing: God still loves you.

When I read that last paragraph, I thought it sounded messy and sentimental, something for a poor soap opera. It's too important, however, to delete. And I don't know quite how to reword it.

The chemical dependent becomes so convinced he's utterly worthless and wretched and loathsome and destructive that naturally he assumes everyone, beginning with his family members, despises him.

Now, dry and clean, off alcohol and pills, the drug dependent begins through the concern of his treatment team, and through the love of his family and his friends (if hopefully he still has them) to regain just a measure of his self-respect.

We must be careful when we talk of self-respect. He regains—if he's going to stay dry and clean—self-respect without assuming at the same time that he's responsible for all this newly discovered self-respect. Other people help us to respect ourselves. The treatment staff has helped us. Our family has helped us and, pray God, will continue to do so. Later, back in our normal environment, our A.A. group will help us. Finally, we may discover that God continues day by day to help us.

As the director of our hospital likes to say: the hospital brings the patient approximately five percent of the way toward recovery. The rest of the process takes place outside of the hospital between the patient and his God.

I am not advocating a life of breast-beating or a wardrobe of hairshirts for recovering alcoholics and drug addicts. I am advocating realistic thinking. As we regain self-control and self-respect, we do well to make similar gains in humility and in recognition of the outside sources of our new-born mastery of our lives. Without that humility, we are likely to turn immediately back to pills or booze or both when we leave the hospital.

I know. I almost did.

5

Life at Home

When I left the hospital, I was scared to death.

For five and one-half weeks I had enjoyed the constant company of fellow drug dependents, and of hospital staff members, all of whom understood addiction and many of whom were recovering addicts themselves.

Now, I suddenly found myself deposited in the middle of a seminary community of 600 people who knew I had received treatment for drug dependency but knew little about the illness of drug dependency. Instinctively, I began to think of myself as a social leper.

I had felt myself to be a leper while gulping my drugs too, but at least I had my drugs to take my mind off my feelings. Now, I faced a knowing world with a clear mind but less than a clear conscience. Even though I had learned in the hospital that I could, with God's daily help, accept my responsibilities for my illness, I was not so sure outside the hospital that either God or I would be able to manage the ordeal.

Fortunately, my wife and my two children had learned much about drug dependency and stood by me in those utterly crucial first days of existence in the wide, wide world. I would be a fool, however, to say that my wife saved me. I must give credit for that feat to God himself.

Let me describe some of the problems I created for myself in the early going.

First, I felt I could never face my students again. Though I was now sober as a judge—or as a seminary professor ought to be—I thought I could not confront my students if they knew about my wicked past. I imagined most of my students were whispering in the hallways hour by hour about my odd behavior, and thought they would confront me either with icy stares or with derisive smirks.

Second, I felt I could never face my fellow faculty members who had only recently discovered the fact about my addiction to drugs. The skeleton had left the closet. Or worse yet: the winds of fate had torn the closet down and left the skeleton standing naked in the open air.

Surely, my colleagues would raise an eyebrow at me. Politely, of course. No derisive smirks. But I had an image of a thicket of raised eyebrows, and knew I could not find my way through the thicket.

Third, I felt I could not get out an intelligible sentence in a classroom. When I entered the door and stood behind my desk I would instantly forget everything I had to say. I would stutter. Or I would repeat the same phrase over and over again. I imagined myself planning to say, "Today I wish to speak about the relationship of God's judgments to the sense of doom in the modern American novel," and saying instead, "Today God dooms us in the American novel."

I'm not kidding. Around and around the two sentences went in my mind, until I finally decided to plan no opening sentence at all. Then I imagined myself opening my mouth and saying nothing, like a paralyzed frog who planned a booming croak but managed only a squeak. And so I went around hour after hour with a picture of an open-mouthed frog resembling me in the back of my mind.

In other words, I had all the worries of an insecure drug addict without benefit of my drugs. I found myself in the middle of what alcoholics call a "dry drunk." I developed all the symptoms of drunken behavior without benefit of alcohol or barbiturates.

In fact, now that I was out of the hospital, I felt that my last state was worse than my first. I even began to get bitter about all that time I had spent in treatment, and all the unsuccessful steps and phases I had undertaken.

Fortunately I had the presence of mind, and by now the humility, to call my counselor, Frank, and ask for his help. He said several things. "You are experiencing perfectly natural reactions, and they will pass," he said. And, he said, "Work the steps."

By the last words he meant, don't stew in your own juices, but practice the discipline you learned in the hospital. Remember the meaning of steps one, two, and three. You are powerless over mood-changing drugs. You must turn your life over to a Power greater than yourself for help. Your life is unmanageable and you must find a new Manager.

I had learned these facts in theory and now had to put them into practice. I can honestly say that necessity had not yet fully engulfed my mind. I had spent a lifetime learning Christian disciplines which I had never fully put into practice, because I had no overwhelmingly pressing need to put them into practice. Now—perhaps for the first time in my life—I experienced an overwhelmingly pressing need.

In my sudden panic I had lost my capacity to love

and trust in God above all things—even though I felt I had turned my life over to God completely in the hospital. I had a "slip"—just as dangerous as a slip back into alcohol or pills. Really, I had the slip that precedes all slips into alcohol and pills. Since I was almost ready to give up on God, I was almost ready to return to my drugs for relief.

As I lost my capacity for love and trust for God, I developed all the fears of a man separated from his Father. The world again seemed a terrifying place to be. Everywhere I looked I saw people ready to judge me, ready to pronounce a sentence of guilty upon me. Insidiously, I expected even my closest friends and associates to pronounce doom on me. And, of course, I expected—in my fear, perhaps even demanded—that God do the same.

Frank said one thing more to me. "Duane, let go and let God," which I knew by now was an addict's way of saying, "Let God be God in your life." Frank repeated what I had already heard in the hospital. It was the sentence I had to hear again.

I had become confused when released from the hospital, because I had experienced in a sober state many of the same symptoms I had experienced during intoxicated states. I had expected five weeks of treatment to eliminate those symptoms forever. I had forgotten a cardinal truth of alcoholic experience: an alcoholic or drug addict is powerless not only over his drinking but over his entire life. His life was, is, and ever shall be, unmanageable. His drug problem is a powerful metaphor for his entire existence.

As I consume drugs out of control, so *I am* out of control. We addicts involved in a recovering process cannot isolate the drinking or the pill-popping part of ourselves from the sober part of ourselves. We are one human being. Powerlessness over drugs must feed into the recognition of powerlessness over the total person. The recognition of powerlessness over the total person must feed into the daily acceptance of powerlessness over addictive drugs.

The recovering addict must come to realize that his bad temper or jittery nerves did not "cause" him to drink anymore than his drinking gave him a bad temper or jittery nerves. Rather his inability to control his temper and nerves (which probably preceded his chronic drug problem) and his inability to use mood-changing drugs stem from a single problem within: the inability, without God's power, to manage his life at all.

When a drug addict lets go, he gives up any illusion of achieving by himself mastery over his drug habits or *any other aspect of his daily life*. Admission of powerlessness over alcohol and other drugs, in other words, leads to a piece of radical spiritual surgery—hopefully neat and complete.

If a drug addict, however, lets go of all pretension to self-mastery, he must necessarily—if he wants to exist as a functioning human being—allow God or some agent of God provide him means for management of his life. Without that power, an addict would literally be as helpless as an infant, just as cantankerous and not half so lovable. Acceptance of powerlessness must lead to acceptance of a new power strong enough to fill the vacuum created by the acceptance of powerlessness.

Out of the hospital I was learning very rapidly that I remained unable in and by myself to master my life and the environment in which I had to lead my life. I experienced the same feelings of guilt and judgment I had experienced as an active addict. I had only two choices: begin drinking and popping pills again, or turn my life over to God and see what he would do with it

I want to emphasize: *I really had no choice*. It's a

56

beautiful position to be in. I don't believe I had ever taken God truly seriously until that moment.

When I went to bed the night before my first classes, I thought I would probably not sleep. I thought I would get the shakes. I thought I would climb the walls before sunrise.

In the face of those thoughts, I prayed the prayers I had learned to pray in the hospital. Though I can't remember the exact words, I know they went approximately like this: "I don't know what is going to happen to me tomorrow. God, I'm turning this whole mess over to you," or something like that.

As I think back to that first night, I can still feel the curious sensation of relief God gave to me in answer to that clumsy prayer. I believe I went to sleep not really caring too much what happened the next day because I had, in a sense, made God responsible for my existence.

Our Lord Jesus, I think, did something of the same, with so much more at stake, when he committed his life into his Father's hands at death. Christ believed he would rise from the dead. But since he was the one doing the dying, he had to trust his Father to complete the act of resurrection. And so he died in a state of trust. In such trust there is great peace, a peace which cannot be adequately described in our common language.

I woke up the next morning tight as a drum; however, God got me through the night. What about the day?

I had my breakfast and marched off to class. I say marched because every footstep seemed to jar the roots of my soul.

When I walked into the classroom, I expected twenty pairs of eyes to be riveted on me. I found instead twenty pairs of eyes half closed, as usual, or staring out of the window, or flickering aimlessly over magazines or book jackets, or sparkling in close conversation with other sets of eyes.

No one even looked at me! Until I hemmed and hawed to signify the beginning of the class period. I then said something quite intelligible about my relief to be back on campus and back in the classroom, and the students murmured casually about their own satisfaction in seeing me back on my feet. They didn't even sound terribly convincing.

And on I went into my lecture without a hitch. I was nervous through the period, but very precise. I probably said more in that one lecture than I had managed to say in thirty lectures during the previous semester.

After the class, two or three students stayed behind to ask me how I was feeling. One student asked me whether I would like to talk to a Bible class at his church about alcoholism. I said I didn't think I was quite ready for that sort of thing. The student said he hoped I would be willing to speak about the subject eventually because I was sure to know things about alcoholism that most people didn't. I said, grinning cynically but happily to myself, that he was probably right.

I then walked right out of my classroom into chapel for the morning service, which I remember was particularly exhilarating for me, though I haven't the slightest idea now what happened in the service.

After the service, a dozen or more of my colleagues welcomed me back. A few, I thought, seemed a little nervous or unable to think of things to say. They paid their respects and went about their business. But several of my closer friends asked plainly and good-humoredly about my progress with drug dependency, about their surprise and relief to hear the facts about my illness, and of their concern for my future well-being. I found myself, wonder of wonders, eager to talk with them about my experience. I had concealed it so long. Now I wanted to share it all in a rush. I could feel the burden of deception dropping from my body.

I taught a second class that day and attended a committee meeting. The pattern remained the same. Most people seemed happy to see me back, but certainly not proccupied with me. They had their own problems of the day and found them sufficient. A few talked to me explicitly about my experiences. And that was all.

My entire fantasy about judgment and rejection turned out to be wildly wide of the mark. Out of fear of my fellow human beings, and of God, I had come to the verge of rejecting my fellow human beings and my God in favor of my drugs again. Even after I had received treatment.

Because my counsel had said, "Let God be God in your life," and I had listened, I discovered that neither God nor the majority of my fellow human beings had any intention of judging or rejecting me. I never would have known that, however, if I had not dumped my life the previous night into God's hands. I believe that, heart, mind and soul.

That night I again "worked the steps." I briefly analyzed my day, tried to reflect upon my many failures—especially of faith and hope—and asked for God's forgiveness. I then turned my life once more over to God. In effect, I said, Let God do it, knowing, however, that God could do it only *through* me.

I have not changed my discipline of prayer for the past five years, and pray God that I never will. Though I do not continue to feel acutely fearful about each forthcoming day, I still know I have no power within myself to master that day for myself. Nor do I want that power. I've seen enough of the peculiar havoc I can create in my own life through the exercise of my own powers. I really do want God's management in my life. I really do want his continuing forgiveness. I really do want to experience, together with his Son, the constant surprise of resurrection from the fears, the defeats, the disappointments and deaths of each day.

My life by now, I suspect, resembles the curve of Christ's death and resurrection. I continue to move up and down, and often down into the depths before returning to the heights.

In the past five years, for instance, I have had my share of vocational upsets. My seminary has been involved in a major ecclesiastical struggle. I have had to leave one home and establish another elsewhere. Together with my friends on the faculty, I have faced continuing harassment, criticism, and judgment from those who disagree with our beliefs and our actions. We have gone down into the proverbial pit many times together, and together emerged topside through that same gracious power supplied to me on the first morning of my teaching.

I have become almost accustomed to and expectant of that movement from death to resurrection. In all humility, I expect God to give me the power to endure, so long as I ask for his power. I expect to endure with a sense of compassion and good humor toward others.

And as long as I keep turning my life day by day over to God, I expect also to remain free from habit-forming drugs.

I say that out of trust in God, however, and not out of any confidence in myself. A.A. members love to say that the A.A. program is a twenty-four-hour program. Drug dependents recover day by day by God's power and grace.

But if we keep letting go out of lives and letting God guide us, one day at a time, we not only lose our worries about managing a lifetime of sober living. We finally build up a hope that God, day by day, will grant us just such a lifetime.

6

Drugs and the
Common Man

What I have written in the previous chapters may seem a strange story indeed. In fact, when I read it over to myself I said, "That's *really* strange!" I felt particularly fearful that my readers would find my "spiritual" experiences difficult to comprehend.

Dottie read it over and said, "You left most of it out." She didn't find the story unusual. She thought I was being shy and gave me twelve other stories and twenty other facts to include—especially more facts about the realities of active drug consumption.

But I don't think I have to, or should. Dottie had become accustomed both to my behavior under the influence of drugs and to my process of recovery. She honestly thought I ought to elaborate further and brighten up the narrative a bit.

I'm afraid to, however. Let's start with the realities of addictive behavior. Should I supply more and more stories to round out the portrait of an active addict?

If I do, two things are likely to happen. People who have experienced few or no problems with mood-changing drugs are going to say: "This man's from another world." And people who have had problems are going to say: "What's he trying to do? Brag?"

As a matter of fact, I was a dull drunk, an unspectacular drug addict. I can't begin to compete with several people I've come to know in the world of drug abuse. Nor do I want to.

If we drug dependents become too wrapped up in the adventures of addiction we may end up in a private club of our own. Like British lords in an old *Punch* cartoon, we may sit around in arm chairs, talking about the glories of the empire—the glories of the last binge.

None of those binges were glorious. In fact, most of them weren't overwhelmingly interesting or even exceptional experiences.

Like armed combat, drug addiction leads to experiences that seem strange or bizarre primarily to those examining the scene from a distance. If you're there in the middle of it, you simply do the best you can to survive. In the process, you have perfectly human reactions that seem unusual only to those who have never been there.

To ask everyone to go into armed combat in order to appreciate a soldier's predictable feelings under battle conditions is, of course, ridiculous. To ask everyone to become a drug addict to experience the peculiar but predictable charms and horrors of chemical dependency is equally ridiculous.

To ask people to strain every empathic nerve in their bodies and souls to understand the feelings of persons addicted to drugs is not ridiculous, however. We ask the same of ourselves for the sake of those who go to war and never want to go back there.

I have written this book to stimulate empathic concern among normal, non-addicted people for the millions of addicted men, women, and children in the world. I believe that more and more of us who have this exceedingly common problem must share the common results with our fellow human beings. We need to get this malady out in the open. Otherwise, we'll all continue to hide the evidences of alcoholism and related chemical dependencies. Addicts, one by one, will continue to slip down their private tubes to annihilation. And families, employers, and communities everywhere will continue to share the suffering, silently.

I have a nagging suspicion, however, that most people have little desire to learn about drug disorders, even from people who have suffered from such disorders. And I don't think the subject is really that boring for most people. Nor is it remote from them.

As a matter of fact, the vast majority of the American people, youth and adults, use habit-forming drugs of one type or another on a fairly regular basis. You'd think we'd all want to learn about the realities of drug abuse as quickly and as thoroughly as possible. We should be chattering away about the subject along with such topics as the Arabs and the economy.

For instance, when a professional counselor or physician in the field of drug dependencies talks of mood-changing drugs, he means such things as heroin, barbiturates, and amphetamines. But he also means commonly used substances such as alcohol, marijuana, minor tranquilizers, nicotine, and caffeine. When ingested *all these drugs* produce subtle or not so subtle changes in our moods and therefore in our attitudes and behavior.

Now virtually every one of us is familiar with the effects of at least one of the above drugs. Most of us have considerable experience with drugs such as caffeine or nicotine.

But caffeine and nicotine—or even minor tranquilizers—may not produce behavioral changes that seem very obvious to anyone, even to the user. Caffeine may occasionally turn your nervous system into a pretzel, but does not usually put you to sleep in a petunia patch, make you fall off your patio and break your feet, or do away with your capacity for honesty and moral judgments.

Alcohol may, however. I have written five chapters already trying to show how alcohol and similar drugs such as barbiturates may change you from a meek and mild Dr. Jekyll into a veritable Mr. Hyde. But maybe the chapters weren't even necessary, because we Americans *do know a great deal about the use and abuse of alcohol.*

Millions of people in our country use alcohol every day of their lives to alter their moods and behavior. An estimated eleven million Americans have managed to become chronic alcoholics. An estimated five million Americans have become dependent on barbiturates—the drugs most similar to alcohol in effects. Most of us have a relative, a close friend, or acquaintance abusing alcohol or barbiturates or both at this very moment. Yet, we still don't care to learn very much about such mood-changing drugs, about their abuse, and about treatment for their abuse.

Perhaps we're so familiar with the drugs we commonly use in America that we don't think of them as drugs at all?

According to statistics released in 1973 by the National Commission on Marijuana and Drug Abuse, 95 percent of all Americans, young and old, believe heroin is a drug and believe that any experience with heroin constitutes abuse. Significantly, few Americans—about one percent of all youth and adults—consume heroin. We easily label and condemn behavior we never indulge in.

By contrast, the Commission found that only 39 percent of American adults and 34 percent of American youth believe ethyl alcohol is a drug. They find only the heaviest consumption of it to be abusive. Yet in 1974 the Gallup Poll revealed that 68 percent of all Americans use ethyl alcohol with some consistency. The National Commission on Marijuana and Drug Abuse has stated that alcohol constitutes 53 percent of the total of all mood-changing drugs consumed by Americans.

Surely all these people know what happens when they take a drink! They know a martini affects them differently from a milkshake. And they think they know why they drink.

These Americans use the drug, ethyl alcohol, for a variety of reasons. Or so they say. I know because I've heard them say so hundreds of times. And I've said the same things hundreds of times.

My friends and acquaintances say they drink to get mellow, to get a buzz on, to get high. They say they want to wind down, or they want a pick-me-up. They want to relax. They want to let go. Sometimes they say they want to tie one on.

Some of my friends belong to a kind of T-G-I-F Club, Thank God It's Friday, and they become mildly mellow together at least once a week. A few of my acquaintances in business positions get mellow to sozzled every lunch period, every dinner period, and every night before bedtime.

I mean that a few of my acquaintances get drunk three times a day and hung over three times a day. In drug language, they overdose three times and experience withdrawal symptoms three times every twenty-four hours of their lives. I used to do the same things— though not always or even usually on alcohol.

Yet, for many years I and many of my acquaintances said, sometimes wistfully and sometimes belligerently: "Alcohol is a drink, not a drug." Some of my acquaintances continue the refrain. A binge is a release not an overdose. A hangover is . . .

With the hangover, the problem thickens. Not too many of us like them. We don't have glowing descriptions of them. Mostly we speak of them with bemused or embarrassed irony. Bloodshot eyeballs are not straightforwardly funny.

With the hangover we begin to reveal the symptoms of the average drug addict. We really don't know why we allowed ourselves to get hung over. The condition is ridiculous. So we try to hide the effects, or at least the seriousness of the effects.

More people put more effort into acting naturally and normally during hangovers, I suspect, than people put into succeeding in their jobs or marriages. The heroic front during the hangover may be a least common denominator among Americans. The great leveler.

America may be viewed from one angle as a large group of very different people united by a daily exercise in group dynamics: managing the hangover with a happy, humorous twinkle in the eye and a cramp in the intestinal tract.

Surely, a great many Americans do know, deep down, that alcohol is a drug, but don't want to admit it. That creates problems for people like myself who want to talk about abuse of alcohol and closely related drugs. Our general unwillingness to talk about such things can make me feel depressed about the future of our country and its people.

The U.S. Department of Health, Education and Welfare has labeled alcohol addiction our number-one health problem. But the average drinker in this country probably thinks he's resolving health problems with his alcohol, not creating them.

So also the barbiturate addict. As long as he thinks he's curing himself of depression, nervousness, or insomnia by gulping down handfuls of downers everyday, he won't care to talk about our common problems with drug addiction in America. As long as his doctors or his relatives allow him to gulp his pills, nobody at all, addicted or non-addicted, will really want to talk very much about our number-one health problem. Everyone involved feels some responsibility for the problem and probably some guilt over failures to do much about it. And when we experience guilt ourselves, we usually don't care to talk much about the sources of that guilt.

Many people believe that the federal government will eventually solve the problem of drug abuse in this country. I've already mentioned the restrictions the government has placed on physicians and pharmacists who prescribe and dispense barbiturates. On July 1, 1975, the federal government placed somewhat similar restrictions on the use of a number of synthetic sedatives and of the most popular minor tranquilizers: Valium, Librium, and Serax. Researchers have discovered—beyond the shadow of a doubt—that such drugs are potentially habit-forming. Perhaps such restrictions will drastically reduce the number of pill addicts in this country.

The new laws will help future generations avoid abuse of such drugs—though most of the tranquilizers and sedatives may be purchased on the streets. I have the nagging fear, however, that the new laws will drive people already addicted to prescription sedatives to booze. I can't help but remember my own quick flight from barbiturates to Old Crow and A & P Rhine wine.

Ethyl alcohol, unfortunately, is an all-purpose anesthetic, sedative, and even analgesic. As a friend of mine said after reading about the new Librium and Valium laws: "Buy stock in Schenleys and Budweiser. You'll make a million before you're 45."

Alcohol and alcoholism will remain with us. In fact, the incidence of alcoholism seems on the increase. And

I can't imagine any further federal attempts to prohibit or even critically restrict the use of alcoholic beverages. Legal prohibition didn't work in this country.

What will work?

Alcoholics Anonymous works for hundreds of thousands of alcoholics in the United States and all over the world. Treatment facilities work for many chemically dependent people. Yet a very small percentage of American alcoholics—apparently less than ten percent—seek help in A.A. or in treatment centers specializing in addictive disorders. Why?

We are back where we started. Obviously the majority of alcoholics and similar drug addicts and their family members do not wish to admit to the reality of the illness, and consequently learn little about their possibilities for recovery. In chemical dependency, we face a problem of gigantic proportions: chronic stubbornness and nagging guilt and willful ignorance all rolled up into one complex attitude. And so long as we persist together in a stubborn or ignorant refusal to face the problem honestly and realistically, we shall make little progress in the prevention and treatment of alcoholism and similar drug disorders.

How can we encourage each other to face our common drug problems squarely, and to explore those solutions already available to us in the fellowship of A.A. and in many hospital facilities all over the country?

I'd be an idiot even to suggest that I had an answer. And I'd be monstrously unfair if I tried to blame other people for keeping the realities of addiction a kind of deep, dark secret in our country. I know from bitter experience how hard it is to admit to the illness of drug dependency. I know why families try to keep their chemically dependent relatives under wraps.

People in the majority—in spite of their own common experiences with many addictive drugs—continue to criticize, condemn, and mercilessly avoid contact with persons suffering from addictive disorders. People in the majority fail to give the alcoholic or similar drug addict the chance to accept responsibility for his illness and thereby to enter a recovering process. People in the majority will to deceive themselves about the magnitude of a problem existing precisely on their own doorstep.

Marty Mann, the founder of the National Council on Alcoholism, has said that alcoholism is a disease that spreads outward from the drinker to his family, to his employer, and finally to his community. And everyone, beginning with the alcoholic, hides the evidences of the illness. Everyone in our society tries to cover up the truth. Drug dependency becomes, therefore, the *grand deception* of American culture. In her estimation, we all become in one measure or another "ill" as we try to avoid the realities of drug addiction in our midst.

I believe Marty Mann speaks the truth. Unlike Miss Mann, however, I am not qualified to tackle the problem on a national scale. I would like, however, to clear the air for some people.

For those of you who want to understand more about chemical dependencies and their treatment, but yet feel very queasy or honestly uninformed about the whole subject.

For those of you who feel sympathy and empathy for suffering addicts you love or like but cannot seem to help.

Above all, I want to talk with those of you who suspect you have become addicted to mood-altering drugs, and do not know what to do about it.

We have to start somewhere. I want to start with those persons already inclined to learn about alcoholism and related disorders—or with those desperately driven to learn. Through them, perhaps, that great "majority" out there will also finally learn.

I hope I made a small beginning in clearing the air by telling a few of my own experiences with habit-forming drugs. I want to go a step further, now, to explore several basic myths and realities about drug addiction, familiar to most of us but comprehended by few of us.

To find our way through the myths to the realities may be something like plotting a course out of a labyrinth. But we owe it to ourselves and to millions of our fellow human beings presently suffering the horrors of addiction to make the effort.

The first myth is probably the most misleading and destructive of all. It centers around your doctor.

7

The Doctor

MYTH I—The doctor knows best.

In previous chapters, I said I did not want to blame any doctor for the development of my own dependencies on drugs. To do so is dangerous for the dependent, and unfair to the doctor. Even if a doctor overprescribes mood-changing drugs for his patients, the patient can say no to his doctor. He can say, "I am becoming a dope fiend, Doctor, and I don't like the idea." The patient doesn't have to swallow the pills.

I have not changed my mind. I do believe, however, that more doctors and pharmacists must come to recognize more clearly the weaknesses of the chemically dependent person. If you take barbiturates for a month, you become vulnerable to them. Whether you're unemployed and on the streets, or president of U.S. Steel.

In the jungle of drugs no man is King Kong. After one year on Seconol, I was no longer able to exercise any judgment toward my pills. Since I was dependent on them I tried irresponsibly—uncontrollably—to get as many pills as often as I could.

Therefore, I have to say to our doctors and druggists and to their patients: don't rely on will power or fate or God's grace or lucky breaks or on federal legislation to prevent the development of drug dependency.

If a person takes barbiturates more than a month on a steady basis, he's likely to become addicted, particularly if he's using Seconol, Nembutal, Amytal, or Tuinal. And if he's using Librium or Valium with the barbiturates, he will "potentiate" the impact of all those chemicals on his system. He doubles the pleasure and the ultimate pathos. And if he's hoisting a few martinis or even a few bottles of beer per day, he's on the way to see the Wizard of Oz. That bottle of beer or tumbler of gin with a ritual sprinkling of dry vermouth—the old Silver Bullet—is going to knock him flat. A couple of cocktails and a couple of Seconol capsules—little red devils—taken back to back may even kill him. Or give him the equivalent of a prefrontal lobotomy.

Late one evening I downed a mouthful of gin on top of two Doriden tablets at the bottom of the stairs leading from my basement to my kitchen. I got halfway up the stairs and turned into the petrified man. My wife found me standing bolt upright, my left hand clenching the bannister with the Vulcan death grip. My family picked me up, like a log, and had to wedge me into bed!

The doctor can't always know what's best when he prescribes for a drug dependent, because he doesn't always know he's prescribing for a drug dependent. Or —and this is what I think happens most frequently— he can't really believe his patients would become drug addicts at his expense. He respects them too much.

Doctors have to stop respecting their patients' power over mood-changing drugs of any kind, from barbiturates through the minor tranquilizers. Doctors have to stop thinking clergymen or lawyers or other doctors— or themselves—or judges or presidents of companies or scrupulous housewives have more power over addictive drugs than all those young people on the streets we read so much about.

I know from experience both as a patient and as a staff member of a hospital devoted exclusively to the treatment of drug-dependent people that there is not one iota of difference between a teenager hooked on pills and booze purchased off the streets or purloined from their parents' medicine chests, and a fifty-five-year-old nun hooked on pills and booze, purchased through her doctor and her discreet package retailer.

A fifty-five-year-old nun told me to say that, so I have. She spent fifteen years in a convent, hiding her dependency in the worst ways imaginable and felt more guilty and illegal about her behavior than the kids who get hooked on the streets and in the schools. By now she also feels a kinship with them that she experiences with almost no one else—except a few professional religious like myself who got goofed up in similar ways.

For reasons specialists do not yet fully comprehend, some teenagers and some college presidents resist dependency on barbiturates and alcohol more successfully than other teenagers and other college presidents. In my opinion, the reasons lie buried somewhere in the psyche and the social background of the persons. The causes, however, may lie just as easily in the background of a college president as in the background of the typical teenager in the streets or hard at work at home on his studies. Addiction will occur predictably as the college president or the teenage student drinks excessively to meet emotional and social needs. Or pops pills on a serious schedule.

Doctors really should know this—and I believe most of them do in one way or another. If nothing else, they know, though they may talk about it mostly among themselves, that many doctors get hooked on mood-changing drugs. And not just on Beefeaters or Chivas Regal. On Seconol, Doriden, or morphine as well. Doctors can get these things. Pharmaceutical companies even send them samples.

REALITY I—The doctor may know what's best especially after you are dry and clean.

Here I will run into trouble with a lot of sober alcoholics and rehabilitated drug addicts. Many drug dependents become bitter about their doctors—especially of the psychiatric breed. Many dependents go for years to psychiatrists who apparently tell them they aren't alcoholics or drug addicts, even though the addict comes (or so it seems to him later) to the doctor for release from his addiction.

Probably most of us would have screamed to high heaven if our psychiatrists had told us we were addicts. In any case, as we think back, the psychiatrist charged us a lot of money to treat us for such things as manic depression and paranoia when he should have been treating us for slobby drunkenness. Or at least for sociopathy.

Also, many doctors obviously supply drug dependents with barbiturates and other sedatives or hypnotics and thus, in the thinking of the dependent, feed their overall drug problem. As I said, I believe most doctors have good reasons for doing so. But most alcoholics and addicts don't appreciate their reasons—especially after they are dry and clean for a while through the good services of A.A. or a special treatment program for addicts.

Finally, many doctors, especially of the psychiatric variety, have assured drug dependents that the drinking and pill-popping were symptoms of treacherous underlying "causes" of instability rooted deep in their past lives. The addict spends much money rooting for his causes. If he finally comes into A.A. or goes through

a treatment program designed specifically for drug dependents, and he finds sobriety and a satisfying way of
life, he feels that he has spent comparatively little time
and money arriving at the state of being he hoped to
achieve with his "shrink." As a result, "shrink" becomes
an exceedingly nasty word in the vocabulary of thousands of drug dependents.

All of which, I think, is unfair and unrealistic. If
Myth I is "the doctor always knows best," Reality I is
"the doctor often knows what's best even for the drinking alcoholic and the pill-popping drug addict. And the
doctor—especially the psychiatrist—usually knows what
must be done after the addict has achieved some record
of sobriety and has his wits about him.

The responsibility for the problem lies, I believe, with
the addict. If he's in trouble with drugs, such as alcohol,
he shouldn't go to a psychiatrist, unless the psychiatrist
specializes in treatment of drug addiction and has a
high regard for A.A. The addict should go to A.A. or to
a treatment facility designed for the counteraction of
illness, drug addiction.

Go to the specialist. If you have the fatal illness, cancer, you don't go to a psychiatrist or a podiatrist for
help. You go to an internist who knows about carcinoma.
If you have developed the fatal illness, drug addiction,
you don't go to any Doc Tom, Dick, or Harry in the
Yellow Pages. You and your wife comb the territory
and come up with the best "booze-and-barb" man
around.

If you're living in a fairly large city and want to see
a doctor, find out the name of your local psychiatrist
who is also an alcoholic and belongs to A.A. or knows
the A.A. program intimately. There are lots of them.
Most of them will either provide you with help themselves or steer you in the direction of those people who
make the illness their specialty.

But suppose you and your wife or husband and friends decide you have an "emotional illness" producing your gargantuan appetite for booze and barbiturates and send you to a psychiatrist who specializes in garden-variety neuroses. Look what you've done to him and to yourself. You come in talking like a meek and mild-mannered Lon Chaney. In no time flat you've turned into his wolf man. He wants to help you find out why you're gulping gallons of booze per week. And all you want to do is keep talking so that you can continue gulping gallons of booze per week.

After some months or years of sobriety, alcoholics tend to forget the highjinks they pulled on their doctors. When the typical alcoholic comes to the typical psychiatrist, he doesn't really want to stop drinking, or taking pills. No addict entering A.A. or a treatment program for the first time ever *really wants* to stop drinking or taking pills. He cannot even imagine a life without alcohol. Or without pills. So how could he want it?

In the hospital where I received treatment, the staff insists they have never yet met a patient who *wanted* to come in for treatment. No addict wants to live without his drugs. Always he imagines he will cut back and down and become that towering giant among addicts: the perfectly controlled "social drinker" or drug consumer. The patient's lack of desire to leave his drug behind constitutes the major difficulty in treatment of drug dependency. Knowing that, you can guess at the problems the average psychiatrist has with the addict.

The psychiatrist tells the addict that he is consuming drugs like a lunatic for a reason. The addict thinks he is thus freed to keep on drinking or popping pills so long as he is hot on the search for a reason.

The psychiatrist genuinely believes there is a reason. So does the addict. And there is. There is no behavior without cause. The problem: the chemically dependent person is too high or too low on his drug to take the search for reasons and causes seriously. He will talk for years about his reasons and explore his past history incessantly so long as it keeps him drinking—or keeps the pills coming from the doctor.

I found it especially helpful to tell Dottie—usually when I was three-quarters stoned or bashed—that I was close to finding the cause for my consumption of booze and barbiturates. Just a few binges away from *eureka*. That's the ticket. It's even exciting for a while.

I think any normal person who drinks moderately and perhaps has never taken a sleeping pill in his life can understand how easily this cycle develops with the most well-meaning doctors and well-meaning patients. In the deep recesses of his soul, the patient knows the booze or the pills must go. He knows he's destroying himself, his family, his job, and maybe half his community, with his drugs. The doctor knows it. Everybody knows it. Including the milkman.

What the patient and perhaps the doctor do not understand is the mastery—the autonomy—the drug achieves in the patient's life. I am not suggesting that the chemical dependent is swept involuntarily under the sway of his favorite drug. People have reasons for abusing drugs. I made the decision to abuse Seconol and Doriden, and I accept responsibility for that decision. But once caught in the trap of drug addiction, the trap becomes its own cause and effect.

I decided to abuse barbiturates. I did not decide, however, to become an addict. Therefore, I could not release myself from addiction by making new decisions or by coming to understand and accept responsibility for old decisions to become an addict. I have yet to meet an addict who made a free and conscious decision to become one.

Addiction is both a means and an end in the realm of

illness. And the patient will never quite know what quirks in his personality, in his society, or in his body chemistry, have brought him into this trap, until others help him to find release from the trap.

Once extricated—once dry and clean from alcohol and pills—addicts may very well benefit enormously from counseling with a psychiatrist, a psychologist, a pastor, an A.A. sponsor, or with a close friend. But the addict must first know that he or she is an addict.

8

The Addict

MYTH 2—The addict knows best.

If most of the drunk-and-drugged population of this country dwelt in the so-called skid row areas of large cities and inhabited houses of refuge run by the Salvation Army, I would not want to talk about the addict's knowledge of anything particularly useful.

However, a mere five percent of the alcoholic population of this country lives on skid row. A mere five percent have reached that state of utter physical, emotional, moral, and economic ruin which characterizes what alcoholics call the "gutter drunk," that incredibly pitiful and infinitely long-suffering human being wandering the streets of America in search of his next swallow of sneaky Pete—cheap red wine.

The vast majority of alcoholics and prescription drug dependents, however, have jobs, get salaries, run households, fly airplanes, type typewriters, and do surgery, while they drink and pop pills. A large percentage are married and remain married, in spite of terribly discouraged wives or husbands, children or parents.

The American drinker is in some respects unique

among the world's drinkers—though experts say we resemble the Irish in their drinking habits. In many countries, primitive and civilized, people drink or consume other drugs heavily and steadily and maintain a constant glow, but do not lose control over the drug. The alcoholic Frenchman is like that, on the average. He may drink from the moment he gets up in the morning. He may have five different wines on ten different occasions during the day and night. He does not, however, drink himself into oblivion. He goes about his daily rounds supremely mellow, though complaining about a bad liver.

I spent two years teaching school in Nigeria and discovered that the men in the tribe I worked with did much the same thing with palm wine. When they weren't working in the palm trees, they sat around all day sucking on the palm wine vat. And everybody—even their wives working in the fields—thought this was perfectly natural behavior. For that tribe it was.

The alcoholic Frenchman, however, discovers if he must go into surgery and withdraw from alcohol, he may also go into *delirium tremens*. That's one way he discovers he's an alcoholic even though he doesn't lose control of his drug a single day of his life. Different countries have different types of alcoholics.

The American drinker doesn't like to drink in the morning at all. He abstains. An executive acquaintance puts down a fifth or more of Beefeaters a day, but he insists that he's doing nicely because he never drinks before 10:45 A.M. It used to be 11:30 A.M. He's lost 45 minutes in the last two years. But he's not belting down beers at reveille.

Of course, he wishes he could. He wishes his wife would let him. And he'll get there, whether his wife lets him or not.

All this means that the American alcoholic, for reasons not altogether clear to specialists, can and does abstain for periods of time from his drinking. He abstains in the morning. Frequently, he gets worried about his drinking and abstains for months at a time, only to begin again, with renewed vengeance.

Sociologists say we are ambivalent toward the consumption of beverage alcohol. Some traditional cultures, such as the Jewish or Italian, are wholesomely permissive. Families encourage the consumption of wine with meals and on ritual occasions, but heartily discourage drunkenness. Children learn to drink at an early age, but receive no rewards for grabbing all the gusto they can get. If they grab, they get cracked across the knuckles by a sober and loving parent who probably believes you go around more than once, in this life and another life to come.

American parents often drink to excess themselves but discourage their children from drinking at all until they are 18 or 21. Or American parents abstain with rigid and hard-hitting propriety and drive their children to grab later for all that gusto they think they have missed.

Some researchers believe that American families prepare a "soil" in which "addiction grows" by being soberly authoritarian, moralistically unforgiving, and success-driven. Presumably, if I'm nurtured in a family who wants me to succeed in life, wants me to do it ethically, and mercilessly rejects me when I don't succeed, I'm on my way down the tube. That surely sounds like a family that would drive anybody to drink.

On the other hand, many alcoholics have alcoholic mothers or fathers, brothers or sisters, who do not act very authoritarian or success-driven. Mostly they go around acting drunk. So if you want to think alcoholism is catching, you might as well know you can catch it from disorganized, drunken, as well as from perfectly organized teetotalling, relatives. It's confusing.

But the confusion simply proves that we are terribly ambivalent about drinking habits and patterns in this country. With one side of our soul we believe that no person can succeed in life without alcohol. With the other side, we believe deeply that alcohol is dangerous and even sinful, particularly when guzzled in large quantities. But how do you get on in life without guzzling large quantities of alcoholic beverages at cocktail parties, wedding receptions, and the annual pipefitters or podiatrists convention?

Interestingly enough, the addict who consumes large quantities of barbiturates and/or tranquilizers is not so likely to abstain from them at all. For days or for months. The pill-popper keeps on going night after night, day after day. And he does take pills in the morning.

The difference supplies us further evidence of our ambivalence toward alcohol in this country. Many experts like to say that pills are more powerful, harder to resist, more insidious than alcohol. That's why addicts don't abstain from them so readily and have greater difficulty getting off of them.

I didn't find that to be true at all. I could abstain from pills just as easily as I could abstain from booze, so long as I could take one or the other. However, if you have your choice—especially if you have a professional type of position in society—you will probably abstain from booze and take the pills.

You make a somewhat better impression that way among clients, acquaintances, friends, and even family members. You don't go around smelling like you just climbed out of a brewery vat. You don't have to hide a half-pint in your coat jacket and hope people think it's a large executive pocket calendar. Or that you're a detective packing a piece in your arm pit.

Above all, you don't have to drop into your neighborhood juice-joint for a couple of quickies five times a day. After all, that's a dead giveaway. Your friends and enemies alike assume that the double shot you just swallowed arrives at its destination.

Popping pills is another story. You can do it in the bathroom while shaving, before your wife ever gets out of bed. You can tuck a handy six-pack of pills in your billfold and go off to work.

Note: You don't put them in your pants lest you get too high and forget about them. Your wife then discovers them the next time she does the wash and has fits. If you have a wife who rifles your billfold, place pills in a Glad Bag and store in the pouch of your jockey shorts. You're less likely to forget they're there—even if you're higher than a kite.

You can take pills in your office, or in the men's washroom, or in any ditch you happen to be digging. You can take them at the sink while getting another cup of coffee for your neighbors who have just dropped in for the daily round of news gathering. You can swallow capsules without benefit of water with your own saliva. With a little practice you can even swallow tablets in the same manner. The trick is to get them down flat side and not sideways.

Pills, of course, pack a wallop. But even if you stumble over chairs, fall over your secretary, or break half the dishes in your sink once a week, you can mumble something about dizziness, flu, chest pains, stomach cramps, sciatica, nervous exhaustion, insomnia, irregularity, the blahs, multiple sclerosis, hundreds of possibilities. I have a friend who kept developing sclerosis for two months and had his wife in tears the whole time, while he gobbled barbiturates. She stopped crying one day when he leaned shakily over to kiss her and showered her with capsules tumbling out of his shirt pocket.

Or as I said to my secretary one day when she asked me why I kept walking into the wall next to the door leading into my office: "I must be getting bad side effects from that crazy stuff my internist gave me for high blood pressure. Call him up and get me an appointment." Which she promptly did, clucking sympathetically.

"We need socialized medicine," she said to me. I never have figured that one out. I guess she thought the government should stop doctors from giving dangerous pills that run nice clergy professors into their own walls.

The next day I called my doctor, canceled my appointment, and renewed my prescription for my pills. As I said, he really did identify with insomniacs.

But lest I underrate myself: I could also refrain for periods of time from abuse of pills and booze. That's the American way of addiction. I could keep teaching at my seminary with modest success, and pursue my Ph.D. because I abstained from booze altogether and from abuse of pills during many academic years. I felt I was a marvel of self-control. No booze. Pills at a minimum, only at night in small doses at bedtime, and sometimes no pills at all.

But just as the French alcoholic deceives himself into thinking he's normal because he *doesn't* lose control over his daily intake, the American alcoholic deceives himself into thinking he's normal because he can and *does* abstain from mood-changing drugs for periods of time. "Look at me," he says to his wife, his employer, his kids, and his mother-in-law. "I haven't had a drop in four weeks. Does that sound like an alcoholic?"

That sounds exactly like the American alcoholic. He abstains for three or four weeks, or even months, sometimes a year or more, and brags about it to his relatives and his employer. But unless he has truly confronted his addiction and admitted his powerlessness over it, he knows in the back of his mind that he's going to start again, soon. In the crannies of his soul he rejoices over the fact. He plans it without admitting the plan to himself. Unconsciously he plots away like a whole brigade of Rasputins.

And one day he has a great and glorious binge and everybody including himself says, what happened? They also say for a while, George is really doing pretty well. He's had only one binge in the past three months. He's improving by leaps and bounds.

That's all George wants to hear. So he leaps and bounds for the bottle, thinking that his family and friends are proud of him. A week later George has been slobby drunk every day and lost an account at the office, and run his car for the thirteenth time over his azalea bushes, or batted his wife over the head for nagging, or clad only in his underpants, the pair with the frayed elastic, has walked in on a group of his daughter's friends congregated in the family den. And George discovers his family and friends aren't proud of him. They're sick of him. He is sick of him. So there's only one thing to do: have another drink.

I don't want to sound chauvinistic. The female drunk manages to do just as well as the men, no better, no worse. If she manages the house and her husband is gone during the day, she may be drinking more and getting chronically alcoholic faster than the average male. The specialists think she experiences much more guilt about her drug consumption than the male does. More double standards, but I suspect it's true.

We still tend to find male drunks funny in this country. We thought Red Skelton was funny playing Freddy the Freeloader. Dick Van Dyke, bless him, showed us in *The Morning After* that perpetual inebriation, male or female style, is not funny. Just fatal. And Dick knows. He's one of the addicted fraternity and has shared his experiences with millions who need his compassionate insights and honesty about the disease of alcoholism.

Maybe Dick Van Dyke will help the world understand that the drunken male is no more entertaining or acceptable than the drunken female. When she finally gives in and manages to end up the day plowed when her husband comes home from work, and leaves the little kiddies careening dangerously around the streets and through the neighborhood, and has burned the paint off the kitchen wall trying to heat a can of pork and beans for her long-suffering family, she is no more or less responsible, reprehensible, or sick than the man at the office who comes in plowed everyday from lunch and sacks out on his desk while his secretary tries to run his business.

The chemically dependent person does not know what's best for him. Whether male or female, rich or poor, Indian or chief, consuming or abstaining, his periodic bouts with abstinence are sure symptoms of his addiction—just as sure as his loss of control over alcohol and other drugs is a symptom of his addiction.

If you have to abstain, you've probably had it as an addict. You don't have the slightest idea what you're doing, unless you know you're going to start drinking again, shortly. And most drug addicts won't admit that, or just won't hear of it.

If you're the wife or husband, son or daughter, or parent, of an alcoholic, don't listen to his or her plans and schedules for happy and satisfying controlled consumption.

Some counselors, in fact, like to put disbelieving alcoholics on a drinking schedule to prove to the alcoholics that they can't stay on a schedule. Take a shot or two of hard booze everyday for several months, they say. If you don't take more than a shot or two each day for several months you're probably not an alcoholic. You've passed the "acid test," because most alcoholics cannot exercise that kind of control over their drinking habits.

Though the reasoning behind the test is sound, I have mixed feelings about it. If some specialist had said that to me, I could have given him a year—if my doctor had me on a daily sedative. As a matter of fact, I did just that. I once maintained a diet of *one* cocktail before dinner for thirteen months *without* variation. I was so worried about becoming an alcoholic that I passed the acid test six times over.

But if the alcoholic is so worried about his intake that he has to put himself on a rigid drinking schedule, then he might as well hear from someone who's already tried it that he's prolonging his agony and his family's and his employer's with his schemes of abstinence.

If you are worried over the question, "Am I or am I not an alcoholic?" visit your nearest friendly and sober alcoholic and ask him what he thinks of your condition. Unless you're outrageously stubborn and dishonest about your drinking habits, he won't have to say to you, "Go out and sip two ounces of alcohol per day for two months and prove yourself a normal drinker." If you're honest with him he will tell you on the basis of his personal experience whether you're alcoholic or not. He can say, "Where you are, I've been. Where I went, you're going." He may also give you a little diagnostic form to fill out for yourself—the type of form used in many hospitals specializing in the treatment of drug disorders. When the evidence is in, you and he can decide together whether or not you've managed to join the alcoholic fellowship.

If you sense you're an alcoholic, don't put yourself through the unnecessary agony of muscling yourself into a mere two ounces of alcohol per day. Nothing could be more unnatural for the alcoholic than this pattern of tortured drinking. But some alcoholics will do it and then go out and get self-righteously bombed, fully convinced they are now normal drinkers. That's what I did after my thirteenth month of "controlled" drinking.

As you can plainly see, the addict doesn't know best. Everyone has to tell him that. I really do mean everyone who has a significant role to play in his life. But more on that later.

REALITY 2—The addict knows best about a few things.

The addicted drinker or pill-popper knows a number of things better than anyone else around him—though he will not usually admit he knows.

He knows that no one will stop him from getting his supply of booze, pills, or whatever combination he currently wants and needs. His wife may take away his money, open up a separate checking account and cut him off at the bank, call up the bars and package stores and tell the managers to throw him out on the doorstep, strap the car keys to her thigh, call up his boss or his secretary and ask for hourly reports on his behavior, or hire a detective to keep him under constant surveillance. And good old George will get his booze.

Spouses have read these facts many times in the *Reader's Digest*, in the *Ladies Home Journal* and in Dear Abby. They've heard it from their favorite newscaster on a local public service documentary on the "Troubled Alcoholic." But husbands and wives really don't believe what they see because they can't understand how George or Mary do it—without money, car keys, and under surveillance as if they were public enemy number one.

But we do it. It's easy. There is always money around the house. The alcoholic becomes a specialist in such matters. Try the living room sofa, for instance. There's enough there to buy a few bottles of A & P Rhine wine right now between the cracks—maybe right under the cushions. And there are always friends who will give or loan. Or people at the local tavern who will buy. And there is usually a hidden cache, an amount the drunk drew out of his account six months before his wife thought of separate accounts. He told her the money went for a new power saw, a very expensive saw. Two-thirds of it went into his sock and hangs suspended in the attic from a rafter inhabited by brown recluse spiders. He will get his supply—unless you manage to stampede him into a program for recovering alcoholics.

Even then he may get his supply. Before I went into the hospital, I used to go to A.A. meetings and then down a bottle of Rhine wine stashed under the front seat of my car. After a gargle of Listerine and a bite into a raw onion I used to float home to my grateful wife to talk glowingly about the salutary effects of A.A. meetings on my life and well-being.

It took her a month to figure out that smell, and the slightly glassy eyes. I told her I was having a pepperoni and anchovy pizza with the gang at a little Italian home-style restaurant after the meetings. After all, who knows what a pepperoni and anchovy pizza smells like? If I hadn't started running over the azalea bushes again, I might have kept that one going for six or seven weeks.

Listerine and raw onion, by the way, has a sobering effect on the constitution. I know there is no cure for hangovers. But the combination possesses some shock value. After a deep swig of Listerine and a bite of onion you at least think sober even if you're not. Alcoholics are incredibly clever at killing themselves. By inches.

The addicted drinker or pill popper knows he can't be begged, admonished, threatened, cajoled, enticed, seduced, or even bribed with a $50,000 reward into sobriety. The majority of spouses, children, employers, and friends of the addict make themselves literally sick trying to do all these things with the drug dependent.

It's natural. They rightfully figure that something's got to work. Physicians rightfully think that when they tell their alcoholic patient, "You'll die in six weeks if you don't stop drinking," that they'll stop drinking. The patient has to stop in his local bar on the way home from the doctor's office just to think that one over. By the time he arrives home at 1:00 A.M., plowed five times over, he has decided that it's not worth the thought. He tells his wife and secretary the next day that he's the Marlboro Man. The Marlboro Man rides a horse and smokes his cigarette with his tattoed hand in defiance of the surgeon general's warning. George will die with his boots on like the Marlboro Man. He's a two-fisted drinker.

The boss says quit drinking or quit working. The wife says quit drinking or quit coming to bed with me. The kids say quit drinking or I'll hitch a ride to San Francisco and become a creep. The alcoholic has a lot of drinks to think all that stuff over. He gets pie-eyed for a full week in honor and respect for each one of those threats. He feels guilty beyond imagination. He doesn't want to lose his job, or his wife. And he doesn't want his daughter running around San Francisco chanting *Hare Krishna*. The mere thought gets him down so much that he suddenly discovers that he's drinking twice as much, needs twice as many pills to go to sleep, and needs another prescription for tranquilizers to get rid of morning, afternoon, and evening shakes.

After a few weeks, he discovers that he doesn't care about any of this rigmarole. Let Mr. Big fire him at his office, the old bag run him out of his house, the pimply faced kid with a crush on Robert Redford become a groupie in San Francisco. They've always hated him. They've never appreciated him. Who wouldn't drink surrounded by an outfit like that! It's enough to make you sick, he thinks. And it does. Everybody gets sicker and sicker. George the drunk, his wife, his children, and his boss.

But George has learned one thing his family and friends haven't learned, and maybe never will learn. George knows now that none of their efforts will work on him—though he will not yet accept the reasons why, and maybe never will.

George is a drug addict fighting against the reality of his drug addiction. His life is completely out of control. He is incredibly sick. You can't beg, admonish, threaten, cajole, scold, or bribe people into recovering from cancer of the pancreas. Especially if they're convinced they don't have cancer of the pancreas. You can't do it with drug addicts either. Especially when they don't believe they're drug addicts.

The drug addict also knows when he has had it with his drug. A.A. people talk about the alcoholic "hitting bottom," or of "bottoming out." The phrases can be misleading. A.A. doesn't mean that an alcoholic reaches a point in his life when he cannot drink again and never will drink again. There are bottoms below bottoms below bottoms. The final level is death itself. A person who has bottomed out may sober up, slip later, and find a new bottom one way or another.

But drug dependents do have bottom experiences. Mine came when I realized I wasn't going to meet my classes anymore at the seminary. I wasn't going to sober up anymore. The bottom experience is nothing complicated. Everything suddenly becomes quite hopeless. The drug addict suddenly realizes that he has no chance for recovery, for pulling himself up by his own bootstraps. He has no power over the chemical he is consuming. He won't stop drinking tomorrow. He won't improve relationships with his family, his employer, his friends. And he does care about all those people and his responsibilities toward them. He hits bottom and the bottom falls out.

No one can carefully create a bottom experience for the drug dependent—though, as I have described, we know techniques by now that may help the addict have the experience by himself for himself. This is one of the hardest things to comprehend, let alone to carry out for the sake of the alcoholic. We can't rig recovery for the drug dependent. That's why so many doctors get disgusted with their slovenly drunk patients. No matter what we do to foster the experience of hopelessness, the alcoholic must finally go on by himself and *experience hopelessness*. There is a horror involved in the care and treatment of the drug addict. We must let our addicted friends and loved ones hit bottom by themselves, with all the dangers those words imply.

Some alcoholics hit bottom and commit suicide. Some drug dependents hit bottom and disappear never to be seen again. Some alcoholics hit bottom and go off to live on skid row. Nonetheless, we must allow the alcoholic to find bottom ground himself. It's like dying. No one can do it for you. When you die, you're alone. When you reach the end of the line with your drugs, you're alone.

Some of you will say, "God is there." Good and well. I believe that. But when you're alcoholic and hit bottom, you don't know God is there. Hitting bottom on drugs may be worse than dying. But only in an experience similar to death—in an experience of total powerlessness—is there any chance for recovery and healing.

If that sounds suspiciously like something out of the New Testament, the connection is intended. Early members of A.A. discovered, with some assistance from St. Paul, that recovery from alcoholism involved an experience very much like dying and rising again. And only the alcoholic knows when it can and does happen.

9

The Addict's Family

MYTH 3—Family and friends know best.

Dottie thought she knew best because she was sober and I was in the bottle half the time. My best friends thought they knew best because often when I went to parties at their home I got drunk and sat on their cocktail glasses.

Many drinkers and drug dependents do one asinine thing habitually. Some people keep losing their cars outside of bars. George parks, gets plowed, comes out and thinks someone has stolen his car. He looks everywhere and no car. He then catches a cab home and complains bitterly to his wife about the deteriorating moral fiber of the nation. His wife hauls George by the ear back to the bar and finds the car thirty feet from the door, but around the corner. George forgot about the corner.

Two weeks later he does the same thing, complete with complaints about the moral fiber of the nation. Since his wife keeps finding his cars for him, she thinks she knows best. But she doesn't necessarily—yet.

Some drinkers sit on people's cocktail glasses. This is a painful experience for everyone, especially for George, the drinker. The glass collapses like a punctured balloon, sending tiny slivers into George's bottom. Even when George is half soused the slivers make a considerable impression.

When George has done this a few times, however, he doesn't yell or scream, but tries to smile pleasantly. He thinks, "I've done it again. What's my excuse this time?" Instantly he thinks excuse. Deception becomes reflective for the drug addict. That's why drug addicts become so clever in their own way. They're ten jumps ahead of everyone who tries to find explanations for their weird behavior.

People do leave their cocktail glasses on chairs, low tables, and on the floor where other people are likely to sit during parties. The trick is to see them. If you're loaded all the time and never look before you sit, you're sure to sit on a predictable number of glasses at parties.

It's a very painful pastime for good old George, the souse. But the pastime is also painful and irritating for George's friend, the host. If George sat on one of his friend's Shell Oil glasses with the football helmet glazed on the surface, his friend probably doesn't mind so much—but even then he says to George, "Shell doesn't give those things away anymore, you know!" And George is thinking to himself, "Those blasted Arabs," and blaming them for creating oil shortages which allowed Shell to stop giving glasses away. The deception continues. George blames the Arabs and not himself.

But then George sits on one of his friend's wine glasses with the long stem. And the hostess, who is also George's bet friend, takes over. She gets this soulful, longsuffering, look in her eye and says, "George, you really have to do something."

Now what's George's comeback to that line? She's closer to home than her husband who simply gets mad and wants his Shell Oil glass back. She says in shorthand: "I loved that glass, and I love you, George, and you've got to stop emptying out my china cabinet. So George, you've got to go to the hospital."

The addict has this all figured out in a flash. His friend knows he's an alcoholic and knows he needs a doctor or some kind of help. And he knows he can't pin his problems on the Arabs this time. You would think that the hostess has proved the point that a good friend knows what is best for the alcoholic. She knows that George, who keeps sitting on glasses in her house, should see a doctor and put an end to the habit. What could be more straightforward than that? And if the hostess would manage to follow up and say just one thing more, she would know what's best for George. The one thing more would be, "But I don't care anymore whether you do anything or not! Because you're a slob!" Or some such equally honest statement.

But she doesn't say that because she loves George as a friend. She doesn't say that because she doesn't feel that way toward him. She doesn't say that because she doesn't want to hurt him. Because she won't hurt him, however, she lets him off the hook. All she says is "You have to do something."

And he says to her, "Theresa, I know you're right." It's as simple as that. When his wife or his best friend says, "George, you've got to do something"—meaning see a doctor, go to the hospital, call A.A.—he always agrees for the moment.

Usually his eyes will well with tears and that doesn't hurt either. He gets tearful because he really does know she's right. And he feels sorry about her glass and about his friendship and above all about himself. And if she picked up the phone at that very moment and said, "George, please, for God's sake and mine, call A.A. or the doctor of your choice," he might even do it for her.

She doesn't pick up the phone, however. She feels sorry for him. She finds him a pitiful creature, but remembers what he used to be and loves him both for what he is and what he used to be. She's all mixed up. She's sick herself with him and over him.

So when he says, "You're right, Theresa, I've got to do something," and discovers a few tears spilling down his bloated cheeks, she says, "Oh, George, forget about the glass, or the whole business," or some such thing. And he's discovered for the hundredth time the value of self-pity. The wonderful thing about self-pity is that it's no pretense for the drug addict. He does pity himself. He is pitiful. The hardest thing the drunk has to accept in achieving sobriety is the fruitlessness and even the hard-core phoniness of self-pity. No matter how pitiful he becomes, he has no right to self-pity, because he is responsible for his pitiful condition.

People say alcoholism and drug addiction are illnesses, and I believe that with heart and soul. But drug addiction is an illness far more complex than cancer or coronary thrombosis. We don't ask people to accept responsibility for incurable cancer. Even if they pity themselves, we don't have to say to them, "You're feeding your illness." By contrast, the drug dependent must accept both the fact that he is sick and the fact that he's responsible for being sick. He's a pitiable wretch and has no right to self-pity.

If the drunk has problems finding his way through that morass, obviously his family and friends have equal and perhaps greater problems. They know George should find professional help, or help from A.A. They keep nudging him in those directions, but they usually fail when George agrees to get himself there, sometime. They think George will really do it.

He doesn't. I told my wife dozens—for all I know hundreds—of times that I would tell my doctor, call

A.A., enter treatment, and didn't. I didn't for the simplest reason imaginable. Any normal drinker could guess if given three chances. I was afraid the doctor, the nurse, the A.A. group, or the treatment team would take my drug away from me. And I knew what would happen if they did that.

Every drug dependent knows deep down inside that without his drugs he will go crazy. He'll never sleep again, never get his work done, never get over the shakes, not leave his room for forty days and nights, walk in circles, see visions, scratch holes in the wall with his fingernails, or jump off the top of the nearest tall building.

And he probably will do some of those things for a while—if he quits his drug. He may do some of those things forever, or once too often. Who knows? Drug addiction is not child's play. Dependents really do have good reason for staying on their drugs. They have good reasons for insisting to family and friends that they will find help—when they know perfectly well they won't. And because the wife, the husband, the kids, and the best friends, feel so badly about the drug dependent's condition, they don't force the issue, at least for a long time.

Out of kindness and love and concern and courtesy, the family and friends of the alcoholic or drug addict do not know best. Or if they know best, they don't follow through and do what's best for the terribly sick person they still love so much.

REALITY 3—The family may finally know what's best and do it.

Usually, if the alcoholic has a wife, a husband, and a good friend who really love him or her, the wife or husband or good friend finally do what is best for the one they love. They say, "George, this is it. Either you see Dr. Philbrick and go into the hospital or I'm taking the children and moving to the Adirondacks where you'll never find me."

Or better yet for the alcoholic, his wife and his best friend say, "She's not moving to the Adirondacks. You're moving to the South Side Holiday Inn. Tonight. Here's your bag. Ask for a reservation under the name George von Munschausen."

Or the best friend says, "George, this is it. I've talked to the president of the company and told him you're a hopeless drunk and a dope fiend. He knows everything. I told him how much money you're wasting on booze and azalea bushes, and how much time you're missing at work. I told him how you blame your secretary everytime you get bagged and lose an account. And he says, see Dr. Philbrick tomorrow and go into a hospital or you're fired."

That's tough on the alcoholic who loves his wife and his best friend and his house, and even likes his job occasionally. There is no way in the world he can blame this on anyone else.

Important people have finally said in crystal clear words, "We're fed up, George. Stop the train or we're jumping off, before it leaves the tracks." And suddenly, self-pity or indignation seem ridiculous compared with the crisis thrust upon George.

I hope beyond words that the normal drinker or drug user can comprehend in some measure this crisis experience in the life of the addict. It is horrifying beyond words. The addict wants to keep his family and his friends and job and azalea bushes with all his heart, soul, and mind. But he wants his drugs more than any of these. The normal drug-taking citizen cannot understand the sickness called drug addiction or alcoholism until he fathoms, however slightly, that this addicted wife or husband, father or mother, or son or daughter, really does want that drug more than he or she wants the love and respect of family, friends, employers, or even God. If he didn't want the drug more than anything else, he wouldn't be a full-blown addict.

I repeat for the sake of stark raving simplicity. Drug addiction is no child's play. It's not like having a cold, the Asian flu, or incurable cancer. It's much worse. Drug addiction is a fatal illness that makes the addict love his drug more than anything else in the cosmos. The very thing he has to get rid of, he needs, loves, and demands more than God, mother, wife, husband, home, job, and lifelong friends.

Remember, however: there is no behavior without cause. He demands that drug because without it he knows he will fly to pieces. He *knows that*. Later in A.A. or in treatment, he may discover he was wrong. But at the moment of crisis and confrontation, he knows he's on the way to the grave or the boozer's funny farm, *forever*. If you had those choices staring you in the face, what would you do?

Try to imagine it. Strain your empathic capacities to the utmost and imagine what you would do. If for a second you sense you might opt for your booze or your pills, you have for a second experienced the perfectly "normal" reaction of the drug addict when confronted with the threat of withdrawal from his drug.

Family and friends—God bless them—frequently do what's best if they love their addict. They send him to the Holiday Inn where he spills bourbon all over the carpet, burns holes in the drapes, wets the pillows with his tears, and is barred by the Innkeeper of the World *forever*. Or they fire him for a week, but tell him it's *forever*. Everything starts coming up *forever*. With me, they didn't have to rent a room or give me a pink slip. I got the message along with them, simultaneously. I went into the hospital for treatment.

10

Why Go to the Hospital?

Many alcoholics—as I keep hinting—don't go to treatment facilities for help. They go to meetings of Alcoholics Anonymous. I did that too before I went into hospital treatment. I believe I might have accepted the A.A. program then if I hadn't been taking barbiturates while going to A.A. No one ever told me I had to quit both.

Of course, hundreds of thousands of alcoholics and some multiple-drug abusers find a satisfying way of life through the A.A. program, in company with happily sober alcoholics. Many other alcoholics find continuing help and support for their sobriety in A.A. after they have gone through hospital treatment. Either way, the A.A. program, in my opinion, plays a central role in the lives of the happiest, healthiest, and most productive alcoholics in this country today.

But the A.A. way may be too hard for some of us addicts to assimilate without the help of a hospital treatment team. We may be too weak and demoralized to benefit from the A.A. program without specialized help. To put it another way, we may be too proud and grandiose to give the A.A. program more than a passing nod even when we go to meetings.

Or, if we are barbiturate addicts or multiple-drug consumers we may never discover in A.A. that the program can be applied to all our drug problems.

The A.A. program makes easy reading (see the last page of this book). The drug dependent, however, finds the practice of the program very difficult—expecially in the early stages of withdrawal from alcohol and other mood-changing drugs. Even the alcoholic dry as a bone for fifteen years must constantly "work" the program, as A.A. people say. He must discipline himself to absorb the Twelve Steps, the A.A. way of life, into his life.

If you are addicted to ethyl alcohol and/or other drugs, your chances for sobriety with A.A. and without specialized hospital treatment depend on several variables.

Have you found a sponsor who is both compassionate and hard-nosed with you? If you're serious about following the A.A. program, you will hopefully find a good sponsor, a sober alcoholic with some experience both with inebriation and with contented abstinence. He must let you know you're chronically alcoholic, fatally and hopelessly ill, and also let you know through the Twelve Steps of the program that you have an excellent chance for a healthy and fruitful life.

Some people are very good at being sponsors. But I suspect that the average person in A.A. isn't very effective as a sponsor. That's why many A.A. groups have a relatively few men and women doing most of the sponsoring for all the sick alcoholics who land on A.A.'s doorstep. And that in itself can become a problem. Even the best sponsor can take on only so many "pigeons."

If you accept a sponsor, you're his or her pigeon. That's official A.A. jargon in our territory. It's better than being a drunken dead duck.

101

Have you found an A.A. group—a particular fellowship meeting once a week—that really wants you and needs you? Though A.A. people often attend a variety of meetings, successfully sober alcoholics usually have a marvelously supportive and confrontative home group where they manage both to unburden themselves and to bear the burdens of others on a regular weekly basis. Most addicts need that kind of consistency for health and well-being.

A.A., however, is a collection of human beings like any other human beings who share common concerns, interests, goals, and prejudices. Some groups are open, compassionate, creative, in response to personal needs arising in a variety of social and economic settings. Other groups may become rather clannish—turned in on their own set of experiences in a special social or economic class. A particular group may share a unique pattern of alcoholic behavior and therefore a unique slant on procedures necessary for sobriety and recovery. These groups may not really care to have different sorts of alcoholics join their fellowship—though nothing can prevent *you,* the new alcoholic, from creating an atmosphere in which change can take place.

The most important variable in the A.A. way of recovery is always you, the alcoholic. And the critical first question you face in A.A. is always the same. Can you understand and experience step one of the program? Can you admit—but what is much more crucial—can you *accept* your total powerlessness over alcohol, and your inability to manage your life by yourself?

As I have indicated, step one in recovery from drug addiction is a tough process to follow even in a hospital setting where everyone is reminding you of the step every day. It may be even tougher in an A.A. fellowship where the reminders come less frequently.

"We admitted we were powerless over alcohol—that

our lives had become unmanageable." Some addicts, like me, are insidiously tempted to pretend acceptance of powerlessness to their fellow addicts rather than allow themselves to experience powerlessness over their drug.

For instance, after a few months in A.A. I became a kind of impresario of step one. I admitted my powerlessness at the drop of a hat all over the place to every alcoholic I met. I made speeches about step one at A.A. meetings. I remember rattling on about my powerlessness while thinking simultaneously of the half pint I planned to guzzle down directly after the meeting. The addict's capacity for deceitfulness is boundless.

Of course, I was proving my powerlessness to myself throughout this whole ugly period in my life. But I benefited from the experience only much later. And I proved my powerlessness at the expense of other alcoholics who listened eagerly without guile, and later felt betrayed by my own self-serving treachery.

Only one man seemed to catch on from the beginning, a Roman Catholic priest and a good friend. He looked me squarely in the eye after one of my little speeches one evening and said, "Duane, you seem a bit too satisfied with your powerlessness. Most of us find it more discomforting than satisfying."

He shocked me so much I had to drink a full pint at the end of that meeting.

That's the problem. Taking step one is very discomforting. Some of us need special help to experience the discomfort. And a pint of Southern Comfort won't do the trick.

That's what I had stashed away under the car seat that night, a pint of Southern Comfort. After downing it I had my Listerine, my onion, followed by an all-day sucker. I came home looking like Kojak on a three-day drunk. Dottie took a whiff and said, "You smell like a peppermint candycane dipped in World War I mustard gas." Actually, she didn't even know what World War I mustard gas smelled like. It was a pretty good guess though.

If I sound like I'm pushing hospital treatment for alcoholics and similar drug addicts, I must insist, no matter how I sound, that I'm not doing that. Necessarily.

I believe that many chemically dependent people require participation in A.A. meetings and the A.A. program and do not require specialized in-patient treatment for their illness. I believe that a percentage of addicted men and women, girls and boys, in this country require specialized hospital treatment and have no chance for a stable life unless they receive that treatment.

Hospitals for alcoholics and similar drug dependents are not in competition with A.A., and A.A. is not in competition with hospitals who offer alcoholics and other drug addicts specialized treatment. There are different kinds of addictive disorders, different kinds of behavior, different phases of addictive deterioration and recovery. There are different forms of therapy to meet individual needs. Barbiturate addicts, for instance, require more complicated and intensive withdrawal care than most alcohol addicts do. The addict must discover the form of therapy he requires.

I believe that every alcoholic or drug dependent who finds himself reaching for the telephone to call A.A. should also see a knowledgeable doctor and find out if he requires medical care to go along with the A.A. program. At the very least he should find out if he's likely to experience delirium tremens or even acute gastritis during withdrawal from his drugs.

Remember: both your body and your soul fight like crazy against you during the first weeks of abstinence —because both body and soul rightly sense they are

104

falling apart without all those depressants you've been feeding them through the years. A good doctor, familiar with A.A. procedures, can help a fledgling A.A. member keep his will united with body and soul in a mutual drive toward abstinence.

But when and why should you go to the hospital for treatment?

If you are an addict troubled primarily by a compulsion to take barbiturates or other sedatives day and night, seek treatment for yourself in a hospital that specializes in your illness. At present the A.A. fellowship is geared to confront alcohol addiction. You will probably have difficulties talking about other addictive disorders in an A.A. group.

If you are an alcoholic or chemical dependent, and you find after some months that the A.A. program sounds too corny or too demanding for you, and yet you continue to consume gallons of booze or bushel baskets of pills, try treatment for yourself in a hospital sensitive to the A.A. program and specializing in your illness. A hospital staff may help you understand that "corny" A.A. language reflects complex ideas in simple words. The combination of complexity and simplicity in the A.A. program throws many people off the track.

If you have a position of some magnitude in your local society and dislike conversing in A.A. with truck drivers, housewives, plumbers, or unemployed short-order cooks, about your common problems with mood-changing drugs, yet continue using those drugs with as much gusto and destructive abandon as your acquaintances from other "social orders," try treatment for yourself in a hospital sensitive to the A.A. program and specializing in your illness.

A.A. does not discriminate against any race, religion, sex, or occupation. If you are a physician, a clergyman, a lawyer, a bank president, or a university chancellor, you will probably find men and women of your status in A.A. meetings you attend. But you will also find men and women of every status imaginable. You share the disease of drug addiction with them, but may find it difficult to accept your common fate with them. If so, you probably need a form of intensive hospital treatment designed to introduce you hour after hour to your fellow sufferers of all kinds. Once you get to know them, you will discover more similarities than differences in your respective lives.

If you find yourself drinking constantly and so worn down in body and soul that you cannot struggle out to an A.A. meeting, but sleep instead in bed or at your desk in the office, seek treatment in a hospital that specializes in the illness currently killing you. It is probably the last and only chance you have to remain among the living.

If you find yourself addicted to mood-changing drugs and without a job and without a family, try by every means possible (even if you have no means at all) to enter a hospital for treatment.

Addicts who have lost jobs and families are terribly vulnerable to drugs. Without rewarding activities and without loving companionship, these addicts may decide voluntarily to anesthetize themselves with booze or pills against the ugly realities of their lives.

With the anesthesia, however, the ugly realities grow uglier, and the chances for employment and for companionship grow dimmer and dimmer. Only in a sober state of mind and body will the lonely and unemployed addict discover whether he has any more opportunities for jobs or for meaningful human contacts.

Many hospitals and treatment centers specializing in addictive illnesses try to help their patients find new jobs and to restore family relationships. Hospital staffs will often place discharged patients in half-way houses where, in a community of recovering addicts, they share the realities of lonely and unproductive lives but work together to find satisfying occupations and relationships. Often a good A.A. meeting becomes a primary community resource for these recovering alcoholics or drug addicts.

And finally, if you find yourself, while attending A.A. meetings, still slipping again and again back to the bottle and the pills, seek treatment for yourself in a hospital environment.

Repeated slips indicate that some part of the A.A. program is not taking in your life. You are not working and experiencing the steps of recovery. If you want to get better and do now know why you keep slipping, you must get intensive and specialized help immediately.

When you look for a hospital, however, always look for two critically important ingredients.

One, look for receptiveness among all members of the treatment staff to A.A. and its program.

Two, look for a desire among all members of the treatment staff to help you gain freedom from any and all mood-changing drugs.

Beware of the treatment facility that wants to treat your problem of addiction to one drug by feeding you another habit-forming drug. Most hospitals will provide you minor tranquilizers to help you survive your withdrawal from your drugs. But in an effective treatment center, the staff will then give you the chance to learn what you have long ago forgotten: how to exist without the compulsive consumption of *any mood-altering drug*—from alcohol and barbiturates to minor tranquilizers.

Curiously, the greatest barrier to hospital treatment for the drug addict is the fear every drug addict has of hospital treatment. Or perhaps the fear is not so curi-

107

ous. Any average, temperate citizen can understand the fear after a few seconds of reflection.

First, who likes to go into hospitals at all?

Second, who likes to go into hospitals for three or four weeks—the time you'll probably spend in a facility specializing in the treatment of chemical dependencies?

Third, who likes to go into a hospital where the staff tells you you're chronically and fatally sick?

Fourth, and peculiar to drug dependents, who wants to hear from a hospital staff that you, the patient, are responsible for your sick behavior? And must accept responsibility for it if you want to get well? None of this is easy on the patient.

I've known some people who died of heart ailments they didn't take to the doctor at all because they were afraid the doctor would put them in the hospital and tell them they had a heart ailment.

If you understand that fear, you should have no difficulty understanding why you, or your husband, your wife, your friends, or your parents, don't want to go into a hospital for the treatment of drug dependencies such as alcoholism.

Of course, the problem is much more complicated than that.

If George enters a hospital for a heart ailment, people don't say, "Who would ever have thought good old George would become a Chronic Heart Ailment? Tsk."

Or they don't say, nodding sagely, "I knew all the time good old George was a Chronic Heart Ailment."

Nor do they say, "Poor Mary, how will she ever face her friends again with old George in there, a Chronic Heart Ailment?"

The alcoholic goes into a treatment facility knowing he's a marked man. He thinks everybody's just waiting for the chance to label him an "alcoholic." He thinks everybody's watching him, and in some sense everybody is.

I don't mean everybody's passionately fascinated with good old George and his problems. Everybody has enough problems of his own. Nonetheless a lot of George's friends and acquaintances are saying to one another and to their wives and husbands, "Thank God George is there, but I wonder if he has a chance."

Some are thinking, "George doesn't have a chance," and they're wondering how they're going to react to George if he does have a chance and comes out of the hospital, walks up and says, "Hi, Tom, this is George."

Does Tom say, "George, it's good to see you. How's the chronic alcoholism coming?"

You see the problem? Tom won't say that. If George had a heart attack, Tom would say with gruff good humor and kindly attention, "George, it's good to see you around again. How's the ticker coming?" Or some such amenity. But with the chronic alcoholic Tom says, "Hello George. It's good to see you back."

Long pause.

"Good to see you back," thinks George. Back from where? The way Tom intoned the phrase it sounds like hell. That may be good for openers. George could say, if he liked, "It's been hell in the hospital. And it is good to be back, dry and clean from alcohol and pills."

George isn't lying. Hospital treatment for chemical dependents is a hellish experience for most patients. It was for me. We have to be honest about all this.

And unfortunately, people in general do not yet understand the nature or even the necessity of hospital treatment for chemically dependent people. The patient, therefore, usually pays the price of social ignorance when he enters the hospital. Each one of us, when leaving a program of treatment for addiction, must find our own way to cope with uninformed friends, acquaintances, and usually some enemies we have made along the line.

But in my experience the treatment is well worth the price. And most patients leaving the hospital will find some persons who are genuinely sympathetic to the problems connected with addiction, and interested in the process of recovery from addiction.

I particularly recommend the parish pastor as a potentially sympathetic friend for the homecoming patient. For a while my own pastor—a colleague on my seminary faculty—was the only person outside of my family with whom I could share my experience in full.

I wish I could also recommend the pastor as a source of specialized care and counsel for the sick addict who is consuming drugs compulsively. In fact, many alcoholics and other addicts assume that their clergyman can help them. When they visit their pastor, however, they often discover something about Myth 4—*The clergyman knows best.*

The problem is very serious. Many addicted people get so angry at their pastor's inability to help them that they proceed to criticize him almost as vocally as they criticize their internist or their psychiatrist.

Most clergy, by their own admission, know little about the illness of drug addiction. Consequently, they make poor counselors for addicts. This creates a dilemma for everyone involved. Since I'm a clergyman myself, I have more difficulty writing about this dilemma than any other.

11

The Clergyman

MYTH 4—The clergyman knows best.

I'm not inclined to criticize my fellow clergy *en masse* for ignorance or misunderstanding of drug addiction. But I can offer some criticism of myself in the role of pastoral counselor to the alcoholic. That way I can be sure I hit the mark solidly.

For several years before I became chronically addicted to mood-changing drugs, I served as a parish pastor and attempted to counsel alcoholic men and women in my congregation and in my community. I knew little about the nature of drug addiction, but I thought I knew something about counseling people in trouble. As a result I produced all kinds of trouble for myself and for those alcoholic people who came to me looking for help.

In order to explain what happened, I have to create a situation with which I am familiar and for which I am responsible. The persons and events I describe, however, emerge from a large composite of persons and events existing in my memory. The story is, in a sense, fictional, though all the details of the story happened to a number of people with whom I became acquainted over the years.

Let's call the tragic heroine of the story Ethel Murray.

Ethel was about forty years old, a housewife and mother of five children, ages ranging from one and a half through thirteen. Her husband had a job that kept him out of town about five days out of every week.

Ethel was both deeply religious and very pious. She prayed daily in a disciplined way. She attended worship and received the Lord's Supper regularly. She taught Sunday school and brought her children with her every Sunday. She persisted in her spiritual life in spite of her husband's total lack of interest in the church or in anything connected with religion or with spiritual reality.

Ethel was also deeply lonely. Although her husband had worked on the road during the 15 years of their marriage, she had never grown accustomed to his absence. She had many fears about possible burglaries, sexual assaults, and similar threats to herself and her children. In fact, I think Ethel spent a great deal of her time praying God to protect her family. Very early in our relationships, I discovered, however, that Ethel had few defenses against the fears that haunted her.

Ethel also drank—regularly. She consumed vodka each day and kept herself mellow to slightly drunk from daybreak to nightfall. When I first got to know her, she seemed dependent on God and vodka in almost equal parts. Together they provided her the defense she thought she needed against her fears.

As time went on, however, Ethel's vodka became more important to her than God. She prayed less and drank more. She began going on binges and sometimes missed church services and Sunday school. She resigned her position as a Sunday school teacher. Sometimes, in reaction to her binges, her mean-tempered husband beat her up. As I continued to counsel Ethel, I became accustomed to her blackened eyes, puffed-up lips, bruises and abrasions on her face, her arms, and even her legs. But when I showed signs of concern over her condition, she always said she deserved what she got, but God would help her out of her mess. I never knew quite what to say in response to such outspoken religious fervor.

Ethel knew she drank too much, but she wanted to believe that God or I, her pastor, or her "faith" would cure her someday. Usually when we talked, she gave me the feeling that she would stop drinking tomorrow. And time and time again, I believed her.

Whether drunk or sober, Ethel never allowed me the chance to confront her with her own responsibilities for her behavior. Or to be more honest—I never really tried very hard. I simply didn't understand my pastoral obligations toward her. I thought I had to give her constant support as she struggled against her fearsome problems. I didn't realize that my "support" could contribute to those problems.

As Ethel's consumption of vodka became heavier and heavier, she lost control over the management of her children and her home. Her neighbors sometimes called me during the day and often during the night to tell me that the Murray children were wandering around the neighborhood, acting in most unusual ways. The older children got in the habit of climbing on their neighbor's roofs and jumping up and down until the people inside thought the house was going to cave in. The younger children often lost their clothes and paraded like Lady Godiva down the center of the street. Sometimes they paraded naked down the street at 2:00 A.M. Something had to be done.

That's what I kept telling Ethel, especially when she got totally drunk and called me over to her house.

"Something's got to be done," I would say. And Ethel

always agreed with tearful moans (literally) of abject self-criticism and flagellation.

"Ethel," I would say, "You can't let little Suzy wander down the streets naked and defenseless at 2:00 in the morning. You've got to get hold of yourself and take care of your family. They need you," and so forth.

At which point, Ethel without fail fell to her knees and asked for the chance to make confession. For some reason or another, she would also ask me to get to my knees and I always did. Then, mumbling drunkenly, Ethel would pour out her confession with what seemed to me to be the most amazing humility and even objectivity I had ever heard from a human being!

Once she got going, she confessed all kinds of things I had no awareness of: misadventures out of her youth, pranks during her adolescence, mischief from her childhood, everything. And I would be so overwhelemed by this apparent deluge of penitent confession that I would grant her absolution in Christ's name every time. Ethel would then quiet down and sit in a chair to recover both from the effects of her drinking and, I think, from the effects of her emotional outburst.

Since Ethel, however, needed time to recover from her binge, I often rounded up her children and sometimes attempted to clean up her house. Or occasionally I called Dottie and together we put Ethel's affairs into a semblance of order. In other words, after calling on Ethel to accept responsibility for her household, Dottie and I took over that responsibility.

Once, while Ethel was half drunk, I induced her to call A.A. for help. A marvelous woman of about Ethel's age came out to her house immediately, brewed some coffee, and spent several hours alone with Ethel. I went home feeling that I had successfully "referred" Ethel at last to someone who could surely resolve her problems.

The next day Ethel called and told me she preferred

me to the woman from A.A. She said I was much more "spiritual" than the A.A. lady, whatever that meant. And like a fool, I think I felt secretly pleased with myself. Where A.A. failed with Ethel I would somehow find the answer. So I didn't even encourage Ethel to stick with A.A. I wanted to clean up the mess myself.

I never did. I continued visiting her, hearing her confessions, rounding up her kids, cleaning her house, and trying to talk the neighbors out of calling the police or the welfare department. In other words, I contributed to the mess.

Finally, one night the police came and rounded up the children. After some weeks of negotiation with Ethel and her husband, the local authorities placed most of Ethel's children in foster homes. Ethel was committed to the state hospital for treatment as a mental patient. And I sat on the sidelines, wondering what I had done wrong.

I continued to wonder for many years, since Ethel never did stop drinking and her family never again lived together intact. Unless Ethel has begun to attend A.A. meetings or has received treatment for alcoholism, I would guess that she is today a permanent resident of a state institution—or perhaps she's dead. God only knows where her children or her husband are.

So much for the story of Ethel Murray and her family. I believe many pastors have had similar experiences with alcoholic people who come to them for help. I believe, also, that many pastors have reacted in much the same way as I did, thinking they were doing the right thing.

With alcoholics, however, what seems to the pastor to be obviously the right thing usually turns out to be the wrong thing. And because the pastor so often does the wrong thing in counseling the alcoholic, he helps to create the myth that the pastor knows best—a particularly damaging myth since alcoholism and related drug disorders are so preeminently spiritual disorders.

But pastors may do the wrong things for virtually the right reasons, as I did. We wish to show Christian sympathy and empathy toward addicted people who have come to us for help. We see their desperate circumstances and assume they need our *support*. Even when alcoholics refuse to show signs of responsibility and sorrow over their condition, we assume they've suffered enough. In our own pastoral vocabulary we say, "They've already experienced God's judgment in their lives. Why should I remind them of the obvious?"

Or if the alcoholic confesses his weaknesses and evils openly, we feel the obligation to assure him of God's forgiveness through Christ Jesus. And we feel with pastoral justification that God through his power and his grace will help our troubled parishioner.

And what's wrong with that? I think you could guess by now.

No one, pastor or otherwise, can help an alcoholic toward recovery through mere sympathy, empathy, or even loving support—unless that alcoholic has made a responsible decision to pursue recovery through persons or power outside of himself. To incline the alcoholic to make that decision, the pastor at the very least must say to the alcoholic, "You need help, desperately."

Like the good doctor, the good employer, the loving family members and friends, the good pastor must tell his alcoholic parishioner, "You've made a catastrophic mess of your life. You have responsibility for that mess. You have no power in and of yourself to eliminate the mess. You must find help in A.A. or in the hospital."

And in my opinion, the pastor must go one step further. Until his alcoholic parishioner has recognized his responsibility for his life, the pastor cannot give the alcoholic any assurances that God will simply clean up his mess for him. Just as Ethel continued to drink when I or my wife cleaned up her messes, so—I am convinced

—she or any other alcoholic would continue to drink if God himself miraculously cleaned up the mess. It would be the best excuse in the world.

Very quickly Ethel would learn to say, "Let God do it," and continue drinking. That's exactly what Ethel did with me. She got into the habit of saying, "Let pastor do it," and kept on drinking. And by continually "accepting" her behavior without critical reaction, I helped to support her habit.

Ethel even learned to confess her sins at just the right moment—when well smashed—so that I would not be inclined, even at a moment of crisis, to confront her with her responsibility for her life and the lives of her children. I did the same thing years ago with my long speeches to other alcoholics about my powerlessness over alcohol. I confessed my powerlessness but was not about to give God any power to manage my life in the absence of alcohol. And neither was Ethel. We thought we could "con" God and sympathetic fellow human beings. And we did deceive some human beings, like our pastors. We never deceived God, however. Mostly, we deceived ourselves.

Just as the chemically dependent person helps to create the myth that the doctor knows best, so the chemically dependent person helps to create the myth that the pastor knows best. The addict manages to stay a jump ahead of the best pastors and doctors in the world in order to remain an addict!

Maybe you're thinking: the alcoholic wouldn't get the better of a different sort of clergyman—the type who levels the addict with a barrage of moral condemnation and threatens him with everything from excommunication to damnation. But the alcoholic probably dodges this pastoral approach more easily than he dodges the supportive and non-judgmental approach.

When hit with the barrage, Ethel simply tells herself

117

that the pastor has no understanding of her problems. "He's as bad as my husband," she says with self-righteous indignation. And off she goes and gets drunk again —this time feeling she has the right to a good binge. "Wouldn't you get loaded if your own pastor told you you're going to hell because you drink too much?" she asks her best drinking friend. "Doesn't pastor know I've got 400 good reasons for my drinking? Why blame me? My old man and my kids would drive anybody to the distillery. And I've got a bad gall bladder and feet to boot. And doesn't pastor know I'm going to quit tomorrow, or at least after the weekend?" and so forth.

Thereafter, Ethel doesn't call the pastor anymore, and doesn't visit him and doesn't go to church anymore, which probably sounds bad. The supportive and non-judgmental pastor, by contrast, probably keeps Ethel in the flock a little while longer—crocked in the flock.

But I don't care to condemn those pastors who assume a harsh posture toward alcoholic people in their parishes or communities. And I don't care to condemn those pastors who assume a mild and perpetually forgiving posture toward alcoholic people. Both types have something to offer to the alcoholic or drug addict. In fact, when a bit of the two types unite in one pastor, we see Reality 4 emerge.

REALITY 4—Some pastors know what has to be done and do it.

Pastors who offer genuine help to addicted people usually manage to do two things:

First, they confront their troubled people with the reality of their physical, emotional, and spiritual disorder.

Second, they successfully refer their troubled people to A.A. or to treatment facilities appreciative of the A.A.

program and specializing in addictive disorders. And there are many such pastors.

Typically, these pastors have learned to be both confrontational and empathically supportive in their counseling methods. They can say to an alcoholic parishioner, "I believe you have terrible serious problems and have responsibilities under God for them." At the same time, they manage to say either in words or through gestures or tone of voice, "I also have my own variety of serious problems in life, and have responsibility under God for them." We exist under God's judgment *together*.

Though the pastor will probably go a step further and assure his parishioner that recovery from addiction is possible through God's power and grace, he will not extend God's power and grace on a platter. The addict needs God's grace desperately, but the last thing in the world he needs is some man's *cheap version* of it.

We human beings receive God's grace because we need it, and when we recognize our need of it. If we never recognize or accept our need for grace, we will never receive grace. Cheap grace, in other words, is really no grace at all. It does not come from God. Usually it comes in the form of superficial or false rhetoric from a lazy or timid Christian who does not take the trouble to identify the very evils that demand God's grace in our world.

The alcoholic or similar drug addict must accept the responsibilities for the evilness of his predicament before he begins to experience God's healing grace in the midst of his predicament.

No matter how difficult this becomes for both the pastor and his parishioner, the pastor must reserve his pronouncement of God's forgiveness of alcoholic behavior until the alcoholic, in full recognition of his own powerlessness over his life says, "God be merciful to me, a sinner, responsible for myself," or some version of these classic words.

The pastor, in other words, must help the alcoholic by putting the same kind of pressure on him which the doctor and family members hopefully put on him, the kind of pressure that leads to specialized care for a very special form of physical and spiritual malady.

An occasional pastor has studied alcoholism and its treatment, and is able to help his own parishioners through the very steps of recovery recommended in the A.A. program. I happen to believe that every good pastor should try to assist an alcoholic who is practicing the A.A. steps *toward an understanding of the spiritual meanings of those steps.*

Or perhaps I'm expressing only a dream. Perhaps most pastors know so little about drug addiction that they can do little to help the recovering addict understand even the spiritual dimension of his experience. But if so, the pastor helps create a vacuum precisely in the area of healing where the recovering addict needs the greatest assistance. I think I should repeat: *Drug disorders are preeminently spiritual disorders.* And like everyone else in a largely secular society, the addict has enormous difficulties comprehending spiritual realities. The ignorant or helpless pastor only adds to his difficulties.

I should go a step further and be blunt. If we Christians, lay or professional, cannot comprehend the realities of drug addiction and cannot provide empathic assistance to alcoholics and other drug addicts, then we create a deep and depressing problem for all recovering drug dependents. Sick addicts desperately need empathic Christian friends and family members who will courageously speak the truth about addiction *to the addict.* Recovering addicts need the support of a faithful and mutually forgiving community to discover the spiritual dimensions and meanings of recovery.

Some addicts—especially alcohol addicts—find that community in A.A. But people in A.A. itself are often unable to reflect successfully on their spiritual experiences. The spiritual or religious dimension of their lives remains largely unexplored—as difficult for them to describe or comprehend as for the proverbial man in the streets. As a result, the average chemically dependent person in our country, even when recovering from his illness through spiritual means, may scarcely recognize the means when he experiences them!

Many recovering addicts could benefit immeasurably from a community of Christian people who share all kinds of failings and weaknesses, compulsions and obsessions, but share also—in words—their daily ration of God's healing power and forgiving grace.

Equally important: Christian people suffering from a great variety of similar failings and weaknesses could benefit immeasurably from the discoveries of recovering addicts.

But if that is ever to happen, many more people in Christian communities must comprehend why and how people become addicted to mood-changing drugs. Many more Christians, not addicted to such drugs, need to recognize their close kinship in experience with people who are so addicted. And at the same time, more chemically dependent people need to gain greater insight into their own spiritual experiences—especially during phases of recovery—so that they might identify with other people recovering from other kinds of spiritual sickness.

To both problems in the next chapter.

12

Christ the Model

Every recovering alcoholic or drug addict has experiences with God's power and grace quite similar to those I have described from my own life. I have talked with dozens of alcoholics and other drug addicts about their experiences with God. If we talk long enough inevitably we find ourselves talking about the same things on the same wave length.

I have also discovered, however, that in the absence of popular models of religious experience, most addicts use secular words to describe such classically Christian experiences as:

—total powerlessness over personal weaknesses and evils, and the feeling of God's continuing judgment over those evils;

—total need for God's forgiving and reconstructing power and grace;

—wholehearted appeal, in desperation, to God for his reconstructing power and grace;

—confession to God of concrete faults and the reception of God's forgiveness;

—daily communication with God in anticipation of continuing forgiveness and renewal;

—the exhilarating pressure of God's Spirit to get out and help other powerless people toward similar experiences of God's power and grace.

When you read a list like that you may wonder why so many recovering addicts do not speak more freely of their experiences with God. The absence, however, of a workable model of religious experience is so acute in our culture today that many—perhaps even the majority of persons recovering from alcohol and barbiturate addiction—do not even recognize events of these kinds as religious at all, let alone Christian.

Let me try to describe what I mean by a workable model of religious experience.

If I experience God's presence in my life, I will probably have difficulties describing my experience in terms which fit your life. As a result, when I talk about my encounters with God, you probably think I'm both a bit fanatic and a little fantastic. You can't find the setting and circumstances in your life which I'm trying to describe in my own. And so you raise an eyebrow at me.

If God, for instance, seems to speak to me in the still of the night when I'm struggling with him for a response to a problem, I may discover that God doesn't seem to react to you in the still of the night at all. And that's the end of our conversation. My experience makes no sense to you, and so I stop talking about it. Worse than that, I get sheepish about it, and so do you.

I'll never forget a woman from my former parish who took me into her den one afternoon to explain the comfort she received from God through a door opening out onto her patio. She asked me to look at the door and tell her what I saw. Unfortunately, I saw nothing but a door and finally had to say so. Deeply disappointed, she pointed out a pattern in the wood of the door which, in her view, resembled a butterfly. And indeed, the more closely I looked, the more clearly I also saw a butterfly.

"Now," she said with deep satisfaction, "What do you think of that?"

I couldn't think of anything and had to say so. Deeply disappointed again, she patiently pointed out to me that the butterfly was an ancient symbol of Christ's resurrection from the dead. When she became blue, she said, she sat in her den and meditated on the door and thereby received spiritual nourishment. She *looked* at the door, but *meditated* on Christ's resurrection. When she had revived, she opened the door and looked out on the evergreens in her backyard which again reminded her of the ever-living Christ.

It was all so simple. But I did not have her habit or discipline of seeing in symbols and receiving strength from them. If she had been talking to a Christian priest in the twelfth or thirteenth century, she and he together would probably have recognized the significance of her door immediately. But her model of religious experience was not my model. And so we parted somewhat saddened that we could not share the power and meaning of the resurrection in the same way.

Now if knowledgeable Christians have these problems today, recovering addicts from a bewildering potpourri of religious backgrounds are literally bedeviled by them. I have seen people at A.A. meetings suddenly contract the St. Vitus dance when they felt compelled by a discussion leader to describe how they came to believe in "a power greater than themselves." Or how they turned their will and life over to "God as they understood him."

125

When confronted with such seemingly simple but really hair-raising invitations to describe their experiences with Steps Two and Three of the A.A. program, many alcoholics, I suspect, feel almost a violent urge to seek sanctuary in the phrase, "as I understood him," and offer no further words at all.

Furthermore, many alcoholics have had damaging experiences in the churches they grew up in. Some alcoholics feel that rigid religious upbringings have made them vulnerable to alcohol addiction. At A.A. meetings, some people will plainly separate their personal "spiritual" experiences—usually too personal to describe— from their "religious" experiences. Religion means established churches. A.A. is, therefore, a *spiritual* not a religious program and fellowship.

It can be confusing. And for a strong Christian it can be a sad commentary on the effectiveness of many established churches.

Visitors unfamiliar with A.A. meetings, in fact, may get the feeling that members of the fellowship share some cultic secret which they dare not put into words. The secret, however, is simple. Either the recovering alcoholic doesn't know *how* to put his spiritual experiences into words. Or he's afraid of bemused reactions from friends who don't know *how to respond* to his unexpected revelations. So he keeps his mouth shut about his relationship with God, even when he knows he has one.

Now, I believe that this unintended conspiracy of silence about spiritual experience among recovering drug addicts really has to come to an end. We have to find a common model through which we may share our experiences with God's power and grace. Or if addicts in general cannot find the model, then recovering *Christian* addicts must find a way to share their experiences in simple and comprehensible and credible words.

If we don't, the experiences themselves may ultimately vanish from among us. What we cannot put into words, we cannot experience as event for very long. Event and word, of course, go hand in hand. At the very least, we shall not be able to convey without words those spiritual events from our lives which other people want and need to hear for their lives. And what we cannot share we cannot forever possess.

Fortunately we have a model that encapsulates our experiences of addiction and recovery from addiction. We have a model from which we may derive words to describe that experience. We have the model in Jesus Christ—in his life, death, and resurrection.

And no matter how you presently feel about the name and the person of Jesus Christ—no matter how delighted or sheepish or maybe antagonistic you might feel about him—I ask you to hear me out. I do not intend to propose Christ to you as a religious formula or a doctrine or a tradition, but as a man whose life matches our lives —as a life through which we gain strength for both life and death.

Christ's life, death, and resurrection fits the recovering addict's experience like a tank suit fits an olympic swimmer.

Christ descended through great suffering of body, mind, and soul into a horrible death. Christ reached a point in his descent where he could only reach out in desperate prayer for relief from his sufferings. In the Garden of Gethsemane, he asked his Father if it were possible to take his agony away from him. On the cross Christ asked with incredibly poignant but straightforward candor: "Why, God, have you forsaken me?"

Very few addicts in the agony of their own downward plunge to the living death of addiction have failed to offer similar prayers. Addicts offer desperate prayers in the face of extreme personal crisis. They frequently offer treacherous prayers for relief from drugs they know they won't give up. Suffering addicts are not the suffering Christ. But addicts do cry to God in words very similar to Christ's in his great moments of crisis.

The addict cries for relief because he finds his suffering too great to bear. He cries for relief because he believes himself forsaken by man and by God. And as we know, he usually has been forsaken by a great many people, as Christ was forsaken by many people. But as Christ was never forsaken by his Father, so the addict, as long as he retains life and breath, is never forsaken by that power greater than himself—his Father who created him.

The addict does not know, however, that God refuses to forsake him. If he is to recover, he must take a remarkable chance and throw himself into God's hands to see if God will catch him and hold him. Because many addicts, particularly alcoholics, have done just that, we have seen in the 20th century one of God's greatest miracles of healing. We have seen hundreds of thousands of hopelessly and helplessly alcoholic men and women restored to health and productivity and gratitude and faith by the very God they thought had condemned them and forsaken them.

Christ Jesus also knew that his Father refused to forsake him. Christ had to find out for himself *by trusting his Father.* He committed himself in death to his Father, not knowing from that moment forward exactly what would happen to him.

Don't misunderstand me. Christ *believed* his Father would raise him from death. But he didn't *know,* as a scientist knows the chemical properties of the human body, that his Father would raise him. Christ *believed* but did not know how his Father would raise him. He trusted his Father and found out.

The recovering addict has much in common with Jesus

Christ. Jesus Christ has much in common with the recovering addict. Both must trust their God to raise them from the land of the dead. Both experience resurrection from death as a gracious gift from God who is the Power of all powers.

As Christ became after his resurrection the incredibly changed and infinitely new man no one had expected, so every addict emerges during recovery a new person—new precisely in a sense and to a degree he had not expected and which he thought impossible. He moves from hopeless addiction to a destructive power stronger than himself to hopeful faith in a healing power stronger than all powers of destruction. And as his hope and faith in that Power grow, so also his capacity for gratitude, love, and self-sacrifice grow.

So the addict follows in the steps Christ made during his suffering to the death and his victory over death. And since I believe Christ is still alive and well and solidly present in his body, the people of his Church, and in his Holy Supper and through his Holy Spirit who is everywhere, I believe also that Christ accompanies every addict who emerges from his self-created hell. And if recovering addicts don't recognize who's working for them, then Christ, I guess, works incognito for them.

Even if the addict thinks he has rejected him, Christ, alive and well, works to make addicts alive and well. This I believe. He propels them along the same route he took: down the Via Dolorosa, the way of sorrows, through a death which seems worse than any death conceivable, to a recovery which seems more glorious than any recovery conceivable.

The story of every addict's struggle for freedom against the threats of addiction is the archetypal story of Christ's struggle for life against the powers of the dead—the story of the Father's intention to give through his dying and rising Son the hope of eternal life to all his people.

The Christian path from death to life is contained, of course, as in a miniature in the twelve steps of the A.A. program. The founders of A.A., William Wilson and Dr. Robert Smith, had hoped to write into the A.A. steps more specific references to God's actions through Christ on behalf of recovering alcoholics. Because many of their "agnostic" friends in the program had difficulties with God language and with a Christian instinct and imagination for language, the founders settled for more vague references to powers greater than themselves, and to God as they understood him. Many alcoholics down through the years have insisted they could not stomach any language more potently "religious" than this. And I believe them.

Inevitably and necessarily, however, our secular sensitivities drive us to disguise spectacular Christian experiences in mundane and even misleading language. A.A. could not draw people from great varieties of religious backgrounds without the disguise. But our secular sensitivities makes us pay a price. In the A.A. steps, for instance, we miss especially those words which would signify God's gracious and forgiving acts toward recovering addicts. The accent in the steps falls on the word "power." In recovery we receive God's power to go out hale and hearty with changed lives to help others experience change.

But as the steps on confession and absolution (or in A.A. language, on moral inventory, admission, and amendment) so clearly indicate, the addict needs not only or even primarily power for change. He needs grace before he can come alive in that saving way described so vividly in the steps. He requires God's grace to come alive with an enduring sense of gratitude for his resurrection from addiction. He requires grace to come alive again and again, day by day, with a continuing sense of wonder and astonishment over his recovery. He requires the assurance of God's forgiveness before he can fully forgive himself. And he requires a powerful sense of God's forgiveness and acceptance before he can go out to accept and forgive other human beings, alcoholic or otherwise.

But again, I believe that whether he knows it or not, the recovering addict receives his necessary measure of grace from God through Jesus Christ. Even if the addict prospers unaware of the means of his newfound power and grace, I believe Christ remains supremely conscious of him, and remains with him day by day as he "works" the A.A. program.

The language of the A.A. steps of spiritual recovery is not sufficiently vague to remove Christ from their premises. The language, however is vague enough to confuse and even silence many recovering addicts as they try to talk about their experiences with God—as Father, or Son, or in any other form or identity. And the formulas restrain recovering alcoholics and other addicts, I believe, from sharing their spiritual experiences with other Christians recovering from their own varieties of spiritual sicknesses.

Now, I am not even going to suggest the change of so much as one jot or tittle of the A.A. steps. The suggestion would amount to outrageous presumption. As A.A. people know and say: "The A.A. steps have worked for hundreds of thousands of people and they're good enough for me."

I will suggest, however, that the model of Christ's life, death, and resurrection stands available to anyone who wishes, as it were, a further commentary on the meaning and the function of the steps. The model of Christ may be used by recovering alcoholics and other addicts to talk together about their spiritual life. The model is available to any pastor who wishes to help both himself and his afflicted or recovering parishioners understand the wonderfully Christ-like pattern of addictive sickness and recovery: from death to life—but only at the price of a death.

The model of Christ's life, death, and resurrection stands available to any recovering addict who wishes to describe his experiences to a non-addicted family member, or friend—a fellow Christian, perhaps. It is available to *any Christian* who wishes to share his own version of death to those evils which would separate him from the Father and the new life he has received from the Father of all life.

Christian people addicted to drugs and Christian people obsessed and overcome with other varieties of evil can talk together about the same experiences in the same language which God created through the gift of his Son. It is not simply the language of the churches, religious and therefore stale and unprofitable. It is the language of the ages, reflecting man's perpetual need and desire from the beginning of time for victory over death.

Many recovering addicts sense this, perhaps without fully knowing it. Some have insisted that A.A. alone in the 20th century has discovered the spiritual secret of the ages: total surrender to God in exchange for the miraculous and gracious power to sacrifice a life for others. In some sense it is "new." The imitation of Christ has become such a novelty in our times that those who stumble upon it out of dire need believe they have made yet again a new spiritual discovery.

If the discovery has been made it should be shared. Why aren't we addicts sharing the good news of recovery from addiction?

13

Christian Addicts
All Over the Place

I can hear some of my A.A. friends telling me right now: "Recovering addicts don't keep their experiences to themselves. They share them all the time with troubled alcoholics. That's what Step Twelve, the last step in the A.A. program, is all about: having had a spiritual experience as a result of these steps, we tried to carry this message to alcoholics."

Some A.A. members carry that message almost as a full-time occupation. I know several people who will drop almost anything to visit a prospective A.A. brother or sister, day or night. And I firmly believe in the A.A. principle that happily sober alcoholics provide some of the most effective help in the world for unhappily drunk alcoholics.

No one can confront a sick alcoholic so persuasively as a well, and carefully articulate, alcoholic. The sober A.A. member not only supplies the drinking addict a tough and realistic picture of the illness they share; he supplies through his very person the hope for recovery.

The sick alcoholic sees another alcoholic who, wonder of wonders, walks on steady legs, smiles through clear eyes, and speaks without a slur. The drunk, who can't walk a straight line, sees everything double, and talks as if his mouth were filled with Elmer's Glue, is frequently shocked into the first stages of recovery by the very sight and sound of his new alcoholic friend.

But addicts carrying the "message" self-sacrificially to other addicts still keep the message of hope largely among themselves. Why can't recovering drug dependents also carry the message and share their experiences, good and bad, with persons who may not be addicted to mood-changing drugs, but may be trapped by equally vicious and destructive patterns of behavior?

Or why can't people who have themselves recovered from equally vicious and destructive patterns of behavior share their experiences with recovering addicts? Especially if anyone involved is Christian and shares Christ mutually?

I am not thinking of anything so elaborate as a sponsor system. I don't believe sober alcoholics should necessarily go out to visit people compulsively driven to indulge, for instance, in sexual promiscuity. Nor do I think people who have recovered, by God's grace, from the compulsive urge to indulge in sexual promiscuity should make calls on other persons struggling in the depths with alcohol or barbiturate addiction. I am thinking instead of settings in which people with varieties of diabolically obsessive problems may exchange invaluable experiences of their own hopelessness in the face of those evils, and their experiences with God's counteracting sources of hope.

Several obstacles stand in the way of such mutually beneficial exchanges. First, alcoholics and other chemically dependent people fear critical rejection from persons not addicted to habit-forming drugs. Many alcoholics apparently must remain completely anonymous on the job or even among their families lest they lose their positions or the love of their own relatives. Many alcoholics apparently cannot tell their best friends about the wonders of recovery from alcoholism without straining the bonds of their friendship.

But when will this destructive social condition begin to change? In my opinion, when more and more Christian people who also happen to be addicted people begin to share their many experiences with addiction with others who have little experience. As recovering Christian addicts bring their lives out of the realm of obscurity or darkness into the light of public exposure, more and more people will understand how perfectly human and predictable and even comprehensible the sickness of addiction is.

To this point in history, addicted people have understandably experienced profound shame over the mysteriously insurmountable malady of drug addiction. That's one of the reasons we've learned little about drug abuse. Shame-ridden people make poor sources of information.

But alcoholics and similar drug addicts today tell each other all the time that they suffer from a bona fide illness—a complex illness of body, soul, and mind, to be sure—but an illness "recognized" by the American Medical Association, no less. Addicts know they do not have to remain perpetually guilt-ridden about it all, even if they manage to do so.

More importantly: drug addicts know they have discovered spectacular sources and powers for recovery from their illness. When they admitted that by themselves they had no power for recovery, lo and behold they received from God powers they never knew existed. Out of human weakness has come, as by great surprise, an unexpected flow of divine strength.

St. Paul had a very similar experience. He spoke of his "thorn in the flesh" which troubled him so badly that he asked God three times to remove the thorn. God didn't. But Paul didn't cave in, either. Instead, Paul discovered that precisely in the midst of his own weakness (we don't know what he suffered from) God's strength showed through most obviously. God's strength "was made perfect" through Paul's weakness. Because the thorn didn't go away, Paul learned to rely more directly on God's grace. Through God's power, Paul triumphed over his own powerlessness. He discovered that God's strength was "sufficient" for him and told everyone about his discovery (2 Corinthians 12:7-9).

Similarly, we chemically dependent people, unable to remain sober and productive by ourselves, learn precisely out of our own weaknesses that God can graciously grant sobriety and productivity. And dare we be ashamed of that power? St. Paul thought not. If we have experienced God's healing grace in this remarkable manner, don't we have some obligations to share that grace with others—not only with fellow drug dependents, but with people addicted to equally diabolical and destructive forms of behavior?

But we face a second obstacle. Most Christian people, no matter how many problems they may experience in their own lives, believe that chemically dependent people suffer from unique problems. Persons addicted to mood-altering drugs experience difficulties of life which are categorically different from any other difficulties in life. The alcoholic or drug addict is like a man or woman from Mars. Persons not addicted to drugs do best to view their addicted brothers and sisters from a distance.

If such differences existed, persons dependent and persons not dependent upon drugs could share nothing. They would be unable to find even the words to describe their unique experiences to each other. But those differences are figments of our imagination and products of our ignorance.

Men and women, boys and girls, become trapped in all kinds of compulsive and destructive patterns of behavior very similar to the patterns of drug addiction.

People become compulsively obsessed with sexual promiscuity. They can't let a day pass without attempting the seduction of a fellow human being. Or they become trapped in an abnormal variety of sexual experience and cannot by themselves break out of the trap. When they come to a counselor for help, they talk of their powerlessness over their obsessions in much the same way drug addicts talk of their powerlessness.

People become obsessed with food and consume it until they burst their seams and frequently their hearts.

People become obsessed with gambling, taking reckless chances with their life support systems.

People become obsessed with beating their own children.

People have nervous breakdowns, and in abject fear, become obsessed over the possibility of having another one.

People become obsessed with aggressive and violent actions. They find little or no satisfaction in life unless they beat somebody's brains bloody at least once a week. They go to the movies and watch Clint Eastwood or Charles Bronson or Bruce Lee, and come home ready to give their wife a karate chop behind the ear just to get through another tedious day.

Maybe these people have the obvious types of compulsions—almost as obvious as the compulsion to abuse habit-forming drugs.

But I can think, also, of people (and here I think of myself as well as others) addicted to making proud and self-righteous judgments against others. Of people who cannot let a day pass without crippling a neighbor or a fellow employee or a student or even a friend with a verbal assault. I think of people so envious of others' successes in life that day after day they die with jealousy over their neighbors' cars or homes, good looks, youth, or status in their communities, and lust after similar successes like a salmon lusting for his spawning grounds.

People addicted to lustful, arrogant, envious, slothful, suicidal, or violent forms of behavior experience as much misery and often cause as much misery as drug dependents—and often they know it, at least deep in their hearts. Yet because they may feel their behavior is more or less acceptable in their community, they feel no demand to confess it or share it with others. And they experience less need for change through God's power and grace than persons addicted to drugs or to more destructive forms of behavior.

Because, however, they feel less need to expose their destructive behavior, they ultimately deceive themselves and others just as effectively as drug addicts who may feel the need to come clean with their faults, but fear violent social criticism.

Whereas, the obvious severity of the sickness, drug addiction, may finally bring an addict into a fellowship of recovering addicts, the less obvious severity of obsessively proud and judgmental acts may prevent a supremely arrogant person from entering a fellowship of recovering self-righteous prigs.

And that's a shame.

I am convinced, however, that all of us suffering from various obsessions and compulsions can share our experiences, good and bad, if we can get together with Christ as our common denominator—as our group leader, so to speak—if we allow ourselves together to follow his way through death to life, to identify with him in defeat as well as in victory.

But what would this mean, practically speaking? I don't want to end this book with a barrage of pious rhetoric unsuitable for practical consumption. What am I proposing?

Should I propose the formation of yet another group of persons in a world already gathered everywhere in groups, processing themselves with yoga, or t'ai chi, or T.A., or T.M., or P.E.T., or Kung Fu, or aikido, or serendipity, or biofeedback, or any combination of the above. Probably not.

I could, however, envision men and women, and even some older boys and girls, gathering together quietly within the Christian community and thinking of themselves simply as powerless people, ready to share openly without worrying about betrayal of confidences their own experiences with varieties of powerlessness, and with their common needs for God's power and grace. I believe that the little body of recovering alcoholics present in most Christian congregations of any size could very well form the catalyst for such a group.

I could not think of the group as denominational, a Roman Catholic or Baptist or Lutheran group. The group should be as interdenominational as human evil itself. Also, people from different church backgrounds, I think, have slightly different experiences with personal evils and defeats, and even somewhat different experiences with God's healing grace. Powerless people relatively public should have the advantage of sharing the whole spectrum of possibilities.

Small groups of people furthermore give themselves the opportunity to share Christ's Spirit back and forth through their own thoughts, feelings, and words. Christians have never claimed Christ to be present among them in supernaturally spooky ways. Christ chooses to be present in baptism's water, in the common commodities of the Holy Communion, and wherever two or three people alive in the flesh gather together in his name. People together permit Christ to gather together with them. And with Christ comes the model of his life, death, and resurrection which needy people may share as a pattern for their own necessary death to personal evils, and for their own hope for resurrection.

I would like, therefore, to challenge that little group of alcoholics and similar drug addicts present in virtually every Christian congregation in this country to talk to their pastor and to schedule a small group meeting for interested members and friends within the congregation and community.

Purpose of the meeting: sharing of information about alcoholism and related forms of drug addiction, of course. But more importantly: sharing of personal experience with human powerlessness over obsessive evils, and with gracious relief from God.

People will come to a group such as this. Some people will be interested in the subject, in general. Some will want to find out whether they're alcoholics or not. Some of these will discover they are. Some will want to know whether good old dad or their Aunt Tille or their teenage son or daughter is an alcoholic or a drug addict. Some will want to see a real live drug addict in captivity—within the four walls of a church building.

Once people have come, the alcoholics present have the opportunity to talk both about alcoholism in general, and about the particular powerlessness over that drug they have been privileged to experience in their lives. The experience is precisely that: a privilege. Through the experience, God introduced himself in judgment (which we addicts have surely felt in our lowest hours) and in grace (which we have surely experienced as we emerged from those lowest hours).

If you're the first speaker, however, remember that your experience with addiction places you on no pedestal. God *gives* you the chance to talk to others about your weaknesses, and his strength made perfect in and through your weaknesses. If you manage a gracious humility while you share with other people, they will receive through you, as a means of God's grace, the power to humble themselves in the face of their own weaknesses. As their defenses begin to crumble, they prepare themselves to receive with relief and joy the healing power of God's grace in their lives.

When that happens, changes will begin to occur in people. Active drug dependents will find themselves asking for help to overcome their dependencies. Persons obsessed with sexual conquest will discover the greater beauty of a life free from the terrible demand to abuse others for their own survival. Arrogant people will find it difficult to be quite so destructively arrogant. Slothful people may even discover themselves finally getting organized next week.

Anything is possible so long as Christ is present. I have seen and heard people share problems which they thought impossible to share, and receive solutions which they had long thought beyond their grasp.

In some of these group gatherings I have been privileged to be the first speaker, but by no means the last speaker. Drug addiction is a fine weakness to get a handle on. The problem has human interest. It provides comic as well as tragic relief—and it offers substance for discussion. People like to hear from you about the up and downs and ups of your existence. Most especially, they want to hear from you a confident word about God's continuing power in your world and in their world. And as they listen to you, they will be stimulated to speak with some ease about their own ups and downs and hopefully ups. It's marvelous.

I am convinced that the future for the alcoholic and similar drug addict of the world could be greatly brightened if Christian people would use their common Christian resources to help the addicted population of the world. I am equally convinced that the future for many non-alcoholic but seriously obsessed Christian people could be greatly brightened if they would in some numbers begin to share with their addicted brothers and sisters the obvious: their own experiences with common human weaknesses and with God's counteractive power over their weaknesses.

The Christian community could make a great difference for alcoholics and other drug addicts of this country and the world. If Christians in some numbers could begin to listen and to talk to their addicted friends in Christ, recognizing with humility their own addictions to other sorts of destructive behavior, a new era could begin in the history of recovery from alcoholism and related dependencies.

But if Christians themselves, addicted to habit-forming drugs and not addicted to habit-forming drugs, cannot understand and share common experiences of failure and of God's faithfulness to them in the midst of failure, then I suspect—and I can be glum about this —that the vast majority of drug addicts will never discover the possibilities for recovery. A.A. will forever remain a relatively small fellowship of people serving only a small percentage of the addicted citizenry of our planet. Hospital treatment for people addicted to mood-changing drugs will never become a commonplace. Relatively few of the younger addicts will seek treatment or enter the A.A. fellowship—before they experience the ravages of long-term addiction.

In the absence of such communication in the churches, I believe that the future for the vast majority of alcoholics and similar drug addicts in this country is uncertain. Dependent upon several factors, I would go so far as to say "uncertain to dim." Though on some days, I feel that the future is "uncertain to bright." You know most of the factors by now.

14

The Uncertain Future

You can see by the title of this chapter that I am learning by now in a sober state of mind to stick to my goal and tell the truth. The future, in my opinion, is uncertain for alcoholics and other drug dependents in the United States and elsewhere in the world.

Much depends on the following problems and possible solutions for them. We have already talked at great length about some of them, such as:

—the average American doctor's lack of knowledge of the illness, drug addiction, and his inability—or in some cases, unwillingness—to offer help and treatment;

—the inability of solidly Christian people to comprehend drug addiction as a spiritual illness requiring spiritual means of recovery.

But there are several factors I have not yet mentioned:

1. The uneven quality of methods currently employed in hospitals and other facilities which attempt to treat alcoholics and similar drug addicts.

2. The tendency of Alcoholics Anonymous to draw alcoholics primarily from the white, middle classes.

And finally once again:

3. The abysmal ignorance of our common citizenry of the nature and realities of drug addiction.

Of course, I have already spoken a great deal about the last problem. I want to tackle it once more, however, from a slightly different angle, because I think our common ignorance lies at the root of all the other problems we face in the future.

I will take the problems as they come.

1. *The uneven quality of methods currently employed in hospitals and other facilities which attempt to treat alcoholics and similar drug addicts.*

Many psychiatrists and internists as well have come to value abstinence as a crucial factor in the treatment of drug dependences. Many have come to appreciate the accomplishments of A.A. So, why don't more psychiatrists and internists recommend or demand for their addicted patients hospital centers and units sensitive to A.A. discoveries and specializing in the treatment of addictive disorders?

There is one obvious reason—a reason to which I have already alluded. Doctors, like husband and wives and friends, do not like to label their patients alcoholics to their faces—especially if they are friends. Patients take a dim view of such a title.

When the kindly old family doctor finally calls George a souse, George may take his business elsewhere—perhaps to some fledgling down the street who has just hung out his shingle and will be glad to take several years and several thousands of George's dollars to discover the same thing the family doctor has discovered.

And old George won't mind one bit, so long as his new doctor keeps him comfortably on the sauce.

Less obviously, many psychiatrists and internists and gynecologists and other specialists simply do not understand and do not trust the facilities which may be springing up in their own communities or even in their own hospitals.

And with good reasons.

The treatment of alcoholism and related drug dependencies is presently in a tremendous state of ferment and flux. Differing methods of treatment flourish, some like flowers and some like weeds, across the land.

Most unfortunately, alcoholism counselors and treatment directors have appeared in all sizes, shapes, and with various backgrounds and qualifications. Some have spent years in studying and training in educational institutions and at treatment facilities specializing in drug dependencies. Others have perhaps dried up in A.A. and have made some Twelve Step visits on sick alcoholics. They have lectured at A.A. meetings, the Lions club, and the local high school, and now have received an appointment in a newly created facility as a "counselor" for alcoholics.

The latter variety of counselor may be well-meaning, compassionate, honest and utterly responsible. He may believe he knows alcoholism inside out because he's alcoholic himself, and he has helped six or seven other people toward sober lives. Which is not to be despised! He has every intention of doing the right thing for people arriving in his new out-patient clinic, half-way house, or even in-patient treatment facility. But he probably has little idea of how to do the right thing in a systematic way for the very sick people he confronts every day.

Counseling, in my opinion, is a terribly difficult art. Providing leadership in group therapy sessions for drug addicts is a difficult art. Just as sponsoring in the A.A. fellowship is a tough task.

Too many people in our country have the idea that serving as a counselor is something like writing a book. Everyone likes to think he has one good book in him—if only he could get organized and write the words down on paper. With the emergence of varieties of group therapy (everyone I know has been through at least one "group process"), I believe most of us think, deep down inside, that we have a counselor in us somewhere.

I think we're wrong. I, for instance, sometimes have difficulties as a counselor because I may talk too much. When people come to me to talk about their problems, they occasionally get a good dose of mine instead.

I also have the tendency to talk with a loud voice. For a teacher, such habits may sometimes have their advantages. A loud voice makes dozing students in the back rows pop into upright positions. The sleepy glaze disappears for a moment from their eyes, and the teacher thinks, "They've heard me. They need me."

As a counselor, however, you must wait almost silently for relatively long periods of time for the counselee or patient or client to tell you in a faltering voice, in a most uncommanding manner, what bothers him. If you're listening to an alcoholic, you're going to hear a long story. If you are a recovered alcoholic who is also a counselor, you will probably hear a boring story, one you have heard hundreds of times before in slight variations—and one you know by heart as your own story.

But if you do not listen patiently and empathically, you will fail to understand the precise personal shape of this man's or this woman's addiction. You will fail to discover the supremely important human relationships in his or her life threatened and perhaps destroyed by the dependency. You may even fail to diagnose accurately the phase your "client" has reached in his or her drinking or pill-popping career. Treatment methods may differ considerably dependent upon your diagnosis.

Furthermore, if the alcoholism counselor does not listen and probe carefully, economically, judiciously, with just the right words in the right quantities, he will not discover how the alcoholic has interlaced his booze with other drugs (or the other way around): barbiturates, amphetamines, minor tranquilizers, Nodoz, Dristan, Aqua Velva, Compoz, Sominex, paragoric, or vanilla extract. Treatment methods may vary, dependent upon the chemical compound the patient has managed to make of himself in his experience with addiction.

Good counselors in a treatment program, of course, are chosen by good directors who are exceedingly scarce in our country. And good directors are chosen by hospital boards who have come to understand the peculiar nature of the sickness and the peculiar methods required to treat the sickness. Those combinations of people—counselors, directors, and hospital boards—are obviously hard to find in a field which has scarcely entered infancy.

We should not be surprised that so many doctors hesitate before dumping their patients into some unknown ward or unit or farm or sanitorium for alcoholics and other addicts.

Until more doctors learn to trust more treatment facilities for alcoholics, we must say the treatment picture is uncertain in the United States.

There are some bright signs. Many hospitals in various parts of the country are creating programs within their own mental health units for alcoholics only. Though the patient may live in the "psychiatric wing" of the hospital, he lives in a community of fellow alcoholics and drug dependents, and is treated by a team specializing in his illness.

If you have a drinking problem, or suspect your loved one has become a drug addict, look for the hospital providing specialized treatment for the chemically dependent person. Look for the doctor who will place you or your loved one in a specialized facility.

Hospitals in various parts of the country are creating programs modeled on discoveries made in such hospitals and centers as Willmar State Hospital and Hazelden treatment center, both in Minnesota. That nationally famous Lutheran General Hospital in Chicago is such a facility. So is Edgewood Hospital in St. Louis.

As you look in your own community for a good treatment facility, ask the director of the facility what his attitude toward the Hazelden treatment philosophy is. If he gives you a blank look look a little further before you commit yourself to treatment.

Above all, find out what the director thinks of A.A. and the A.A. program. Any treatment method involving in some way or another the discoveries and the fellowship of A.A. will offer you, the alcoholic, or your loved one, the alcoholic, an excellent chance for a soberly satisfying life.

I will still have to say that the future looks uncertain for the alcoholic who wants hospital treatment. I will not say it's dim however—merely uncertain. Many doctors and many hospitals are hard at work in the field, and learning more every day. And more and more doctors are becoming sympathetic to the discoveries of A.A.

2. *The tendency of Alcoholics Anonymous to draw alcoholics primarily from the white, middle classes.*

I must be very careful, now, that I don't anger participants in the A.A. fellowship, many of whom may be good friends.

So I'll be the first to say it. A.A. draws a large number of so-called "blue collar" workers from that economic class occupied by people with blue collars. When I speak of the white, middle class, I include the "workers."

A.A. draws a smattering of blacks into the fellowship. There are in every large city of this country A.A. meetings made up primarily of black participants in the program.

Some blacks, however, will also be the first to tell you —sometimes with considerable animosity—that A.A. is a white man's program for rehabilitation. And a rich white man's program at that.

I have discovered from Central Services personnel of A.A. in my own city that a startlingly small number of black drug dependents become involved in A.A., considering the depressingly large number of blacks wrestling with drug problems in the large cities of our troubled land.

Having once analyzed the possibilities of establishing a counseling service in a large housing "project" in the black area of a major city, I believe I understand to some degree why many black counselors attempting to help black alcoholics may get angry at A.A.

Sobering up on the A.A. program requires, I believe, a relatively high degree of motivation for sobriety. Motivation for sobriety requires relatively stable opportunities for employment and advancement on the job. Motivation for sobriety requires relatively stable opportunities for a settled family life.

Now, I am not for one moment suggesting that all white, middle-class alcoholics come into A.A. with great jobs and rosy family backgrounds. Many come in having just lost the sixth job in their career, and perhaps the second or third wife or husband.

But the white alcoholic has a better chance of finding another job than his black counterpart. As a consequence, he will probably be more strongly motivated to find another job after he has sobered up—or to get his old one back. The white alcoholic probably has a better chance of rebuilding his family than the black alcoholic. His total environment—no matter how grotesque his personal collapse—is usually more stable. On the average, therefore, his motivation toward sobriety will be greater. Which means, simply: his motivation to get on the A.A. program or to enter a treatment facility will be higher.

Since the A.A. program requires self-motivation, the disadvantaged blacks in this country are penalized by the very nature of the program. A.A. works best with blacks whose jobs and families are secure. For the large numbers of blacks chronically unemployed and living without the support of loving family members, A.A. can become an insult. If I am powerless over my social and economic situation in life, how can I care if I'm also powerless over a drug or two? Why not drink or pop pills to forget about my abysmal situation in life?

What applies to disadvantaged blacks applies also to any person who finds himself unmotivated to escape from drug addiction. Obviously many poor white people suffer from the same condition. And curiously enough, we're discovering more and more addicted teenagers today who get themselves hooked with the same sense of abandonment and hopelessness.

Almost all teenage addicts I have known have insisted, no matter how wealthy and secure their families seemed to be, that they feverishly consumed drugs because they had nothing else "interesting" to do.

As teenagers find themselves lacking a traditional sense of vocation or purpose in life, they will turn more and more frequently to the mood-changer of their choice: usually alcohol mixed with a variety of pills and with marijuana. Most teenage drug dependents in the United States are multiple drug abusers.

Almost all teenagers, like many blacks in this country, find it hard to take the A.A. program seriously. Or even an entire treatment program in a hospital specializing in their illness.

Until we find the ways—either through A.A. or side by side with A.A.—of reaching those people within our society who presently lack reasons for pursuing sobriety, we shall have to say that the future for the majority of alcoholics and similar drug addicts is uncertain to dim in this country.

Perhaps there is no effective treatment for chemically dependent people who really—deep down inside and through and through—want no help. People determined to commit suicide are hard to stop.

3. *The abysmal ignorance of our common citizenry of the nature and realities of drug addiction.*

The ignorance of our general population in America about the most elementary aspects of chemical dependency is both abysmal and ridiculous. I should repeat some facts we've already shared.

About 11,000,000 people in this country are chronic alcoholics. Millions more are heavy "problem drinkers."

About 5,000,000 people are addicted to barbiturates or similar types of sedatives.

Just about every one of us in this country has an alcoholic relative or friend, a mother or an aunt doped up for years on barbiturates and tranquilizers, a father or an uncle sozzled on a daily ration of sauce.

How can so many people who know so many alcoholics and other drug addicts fail to understand—or fail to want to understand—the nature of the illness or drug addiction? And fail to respond empathically and therapeutically?

How can so many people continue to insist that alcohol is not a drug? When they probably use the drug

153

themselves, or see drugged alcoholics all around them every day of their lives.

I have tried already to offer a variety of reasons. I have only to mention, in conclusion, the most obvious and perhaps the most important of all:

Drinking Americans are *afraid* to call the drug of their choice a drug. Americans use, or better yet demand, ethyl alcohol on so many occasions in our society that the average drinking citizen (about 100,000,000 strong) simply does not like to be told he's taking a drug when he drinks. While he's drinking at the dinner table. Or over lunch with his best customers. Or at the daily or weekly cocktail "party." Or with the football games on TV. Or with The Waltons. Or with his nightcap. Or at Holy Communion.

We don't like the word, "drug." We dislike it especially since we thought we learned so much about drugs such as marijuana and LSD in the last 1960s.

Drugs conjure up visions of barefoot and dirty boys and girls dressed in burlap and Buddhist medallions. And here we are, only mildly smashed, sitting in a Brooks Brothers suit at the best restaurant in town, with a portfolio managed by Merril, Lynch, Pierce, Fenner & Smith. Are we going to say to our friends and to our potential customers: "How about another round of ethyl alcohol? Our favorite drug?"

Not on your life.

We Americans have a long way to go before we admit that alcohol drugs the systems just as surely as heroin, cocaine, or barbiturate capsules.

For too many Americans such an admission would be tantamount to confessing the problem of drug dependency—of addiction.

For too many Americans such an admission would require immediate efforts at restraint with, or withdrawal from, alcohol.

To admit that alcohol is a drug would produce something like a panic, I suppose, among a large portion of the American population. That's why so many otherwise rational and intelligent people are genuinely happy when their kids turn to booze and not to pot.

To overcome that panic and fear, many people say we need massive educational programs for normal people who use alcohol but do not wish (because they are afraid) to know how and why it can be abused by people like themselves.

But to introduce massive educational programs we must also introduce massive amounts of money. Realistically—especially with an unstable economy—we cannot expect such amounts to appear among us. Rather, we must rely largely on increased communication between recovering drug addicts and the common man or woman not addicted to habit-forming drugs. We must rely on increased communication between doctors, counselors, and pastors active in the field of drug addiction, and the common man and woman. We must communicate on the streets, in the neighborhood taverns, within our family circles, at the cocktail parties, at the office, in the myriads of settings in our society where people, young and old, gather to talk and often to drink.

And to repeat one of my deepest convictions and fondest dreams: the Christian community in this country provides an obvious place for communication to begin. If drug addiction is primarily a spiritual disorder requiring spiritual resources for recovery, committed Christian people should be better equipped than anyone else in our country to understand by instinct the nature of the sickness and its treatment.

To provide the possibilities for exchange of experience in our society, many more recovering alcoholics and similar drug addicts must discover a capacity to share themselves with others not addicted to drugs. If those of us who have experienced addiction and have known the joys of recovery are afraid to stand up and say so, I can hardly blame my neighbors for continuing to believe that alcoholics are moral degenerates by nature, or that alcoholism is a malady reserved for people in tattered clothing eating soup in a Salvation Army mission.

I have great respect for persons such as Mercedes McCambridge, and Dick Van Dyke, and former Senator Harold Hughes, who have not only revealed their problems with alcoholism, but have united with others to make their experiences beneficial for the millions of alcoholics and their family members who don't know what's happened to them.

Because a few people have been willing to talk freely about their own experiences with the disease of alcoholism, I believe the American people have a better chance at comprehending the nature of the disease. We have an enormous amount of scientific data on drug addiction to share with other people. Now, we need persons who will combine their own experiences with the data and allow the public a peek into what has heretofore been a no-man's land.

Ultimately, the future of therapeutic work among alcoholics and other drug addicts depends upon the people's responsiveness to the need for that work. Their responsiveness, I believe, depends in turn on public understanding of the illness. We no longer look on tubercular people as lepers. In fact, we no longer look on lepers as lepers. I hope and pray that one day we no longer look on the drug addict as a social leper either.

If we have finally come to understand that the addict's socially unacceptable behavior is one of the high-water symptoms of his sickness, we shall begin to provide him the kind of help and treatment he requires for recovery. Or if we recognize he doesn't want to recover, we shall at least know why. And we can then thank God life hasn't brought us the same calamities.

The future for the alcoholic and drug addict of the world is uncertain. There are so many addicts and so few people committed to help them.

But remarkable advances have been made in the past forty years, primarily through the foundation of A.A., the establishment of several great university centers for studies in alcoholism and related disorders, and the emergence of specialized in-patient treatment facilities.

If we do not lose our nerve, we should continue to see further advances. We should look forward to the day when:

—no one has to drink himself into a sloppily chronic alcoholic of fifty-five or so before finally seeking help and treatment.

—no one has to get a grand case of the horrors and instant deception when he discovers that a member of his family is dependent on drugs. But he can take his loved one to a specialist in drug dependency and find help.

—no one has to travel five hundred miles to find one doctor or counselor specializing in the treatment of alcoholism.

—no one has to despair of God's and man's help when he reads one of those ubiquitous diagnostic charts (you find them appearing regularly in half the magazines on the news stands) and realizes that he is alcoholic and probably has been for a few years.

—no one has to lose his job and cheat his employer out of time and money through regular absenteeism and hangovers. Someone could devote a whole book to the progress made by large companies in this vital area.

Everybody likes to knock the United States Post Office. I wonder how many people know that the U.S. Post Office has one of the most intelligent and humane programs for alcoholic employees ever created in this country. It may be worth the price of an airmail stamp.

And finally, my own dream, shared by at least a few others: No one has to hide his illness after he has experienced some relief from it. I couldn't hide. About four hundred people, give or take a few, discovered the facts in the school I taught. Nobody believed I had been in the hospital for a five-week checkup for gastritis. Or high blood pressure. Those interested in my welfare discovered the facts and prayed for my recovery.

In recent years, I've never regretted my "exposure." It has allowed me to be myself among my friends—an addict committed to abstinence—and provided me many opportunities to help others, some of them also my close friends. My experiences with addiction have also—miracle of miracles—expanded and deepened my understanding and experience of the Christian faith and hope.

I look forward to the day when the wraps are off this dread disease. The truth about drug dependency is by no means as hideous or as ludicrous as most of us have been led to believe down through the ages. God has known about it all along, and has found the way to forgive and heal myriads of our addicted brothers and sisters in the past.

Now, our turn has come.

The Twelve Steps

ONE—We admitted we were powerless over alcohol—that our lives had become unmanageable.

TWO—Came to believe that a Power greater than ourselves could restore us to sanity.

THREE—Made a decision to turn our will and our lives over to the care of God *as we understood Him.*

FOUR—Made a searching and fearless moral inventory of ourselves.

FIVE—Admitted to God, to ourselves, and to another human being the exact nature of our wrongs.

SIX—Were entirely ready to have God remove all these defects of character.

SEVEN—Humbly asked Him to remove our shortcomings.

EIGHT—Made a list of all persons we had harmed, and became willing to make amends to them all.

NINE—Made direct amends to such people wherever possible, except when to do so would injure them or others.

TEN—Continued to take personal inventory and when we were wrong promptly admitted it.

ELEVEN—Sought through prayer and meditation to improve our conscious contact with God *as we understood Him,* praying only for knowledge of His will for us and the power to carry that out.

TWELVE—Having had a spiritual awakening as the result of these steps, we tried to carry this message to alcoholics, and to practice these principles in all our affairs.